ARISE

AND MAKE

A DIFFERENCE

The Drive Behind Success

Vincent Lawer Domaley

ISBN: 978 – 9988 – 2 – 9605 – 6

FOREWORD

No single human being is on this planet to play a small game. We all arrived here fully loaded and dangerously armed to take part in the big game. But it is quite so sad the cemeteries are full of millionaires who died as paupers; great musicians who never composed a song; bestselling authors who never wrote a book; amazing preachers who never preached any sermon. In fact, in the cemeteries you will find business geniuses who never started any company, all because they gave their fears the permission to freeze them up.

Your story, however, is different because you are holding a gem in your hands and this hopefully marks the beginning of the life you were born to live. I feel like screaming because your new dawn is here and now your new life unfolds. William Ellery Channing once said, *"In the best books, great men talk to us, give us their most precious thoughts, and pour their souls into ours. God be thanked for books; they are the voices of the distant and the dead, and make us heirs of the spiritual life of past ages. Books are true levelers. They give to all, who will faithfully use them, the society, the spiritual presence of the best and greatest of our race."*

As though, people will still miss this great secret so Roy L. Smith decided to say the same thing in a plain language and this is what he said, *"A good book contains more real wealth than a good bank."*

Arise and Make a Difference; the Drive Behind Success

And these are the evidences, all the men and women that have changed the world were all great readers but you know what? Among the several books they read, one or two stood out as the force of power behind their freedom, both financially and spiritually.

For instance, Anthony Robbins has read about seven hundred books years back but he said the one that stirred up the lying giant in him was *Psycho-Cybernetics by Maxwell Maltz*. Then, the *Greatest Salesman in the world by Og Mandino* turned a pauper, J.W Marriott into a multimillionaire. And then, *Think and Grow Rich by Napoleon Hill* did just same for W. Clement Stone and Bill Gate.

Listen, what you are holding in your hands isn't only more than a book but also more than a bank. Dig out all the jewels it contains because the time to *"Arise and make a difference"* is now!

Samuel Narh Adjovu
Author of the bestseller, *Dare to Differ.*

DEDICATION

The advocate, the Holy Spirit had been my inspiration all through this journey of writing this book. To Him I dedicate this book. This book is also dedicated to my family, friends, and all the readers of it, especially you.

ACKNOWLEDGMENT

This book would not be complete without expressing my sincere gratitude to God for endowing me with wisdom, knowledge, and understanding and guiding me with the Holy Spirit to finally publish this book.

My special appreciation goes to my uncle, Mr. Samuel Narh Adjovu for helping me discover the potential in me which led to the writing of this book. I am very grateful uncle. I will not forget the consistent support and encouragement from my wife, Rosemond Kai-Mansah Larteh. Of course, my family and friends cannot be left unacknowledged. They have been good and supportive.

My final appreciation goes to my lectures who helped me in any way. Not forgetting the mentorship of Prof. Emmanuel Kofi Gyimah and Prof. Paul Dela Ahiatrogah, all from the College of Distance Education (CoDE), University of Cape Coast. God bless you all.

TABLE OF CONTENTS

Arise and Make a Difference; the Drive Behind Success

Arise and Make a Difference; the Drive Behind Success

Arise and Make a Difference; the Drive Behind Success

INTRODUCTION

Life is not about finding yourself, it's about creating yourself. Those who got what they have now took action now. Time is always ticking, make the move now! Now is the only moment you can make that decision. Don't give up! Move on! Train more! You only have one move left. Never give up! Now is the time to get that dream home, car, project, business, job, education that you've been looking for. You are a thoroughly good person. You deserve a wonderful life, full of success, happiness, joy, and excitement.

You are the only one to fill that vacancy, don't delay any longer. Go fill it now! You are entitled to have happy relationships, excellent health, meaningful work, and financial independence. These are your birthright. This is what your life is meant to include. You are engineered for success and designed to have high levels of self-esteem, self-respect, and personal pride. You are extraordinary; there has never been anyone exactly like you in all the history of mankind on earth.

You have absolutely amazing untapped talents and abilities that, when properly unleashed and applied, can bring you everything you could ever want in life. You are living at the greatest time in all of human history. You are surrounded by abundant opportunities that you can take advantage of to realize your dreams. The only real limits on what you can be, do, or have are the limits you place on yourself by your own thinking. Your future is virtually unlimited. In this book I will introduce you into very

Arise and Make a Difference; the Drive Behind Success

important and exciting topics that will an indelible mark on you once you finish reading.

There is a popular saying that "if you are born in a garage does not mean you are a car". That's such a profound and educative statement. This simply means that whoever you will become in life is not determined by your destination. God created each and every one of us differently and He expect us all to make a unique difference in life. You and I have been crafted into life not to fail but rather to make a huge difference and become successful. Making a difference in life is a strong drive that trigger success. This book entitled *"Arise and Make a Difference; the Drive Behind Success,* will therefore elucidate some of these drives that will help you to also become successful in life. Stay put and enjoy the reading.

Making a difference in life is like a huge mansion with numerous doors. Each door has specific key to open it. Having journey through the overview of making the difference, permit me to seek your indulgence to peruse through the various keys upon which the tittle of this book; ***ARISE AND MAKE A DIFFERENCE; The Drive Behind Success*** is based on.

CHAPTER ONE

THE KEY OF BELIEVE

"You only have to believe that you can succeed, that you can be whatever your heart desires, be willing to work for it, and you can have it"
Oprah Winfrey

The Apostle Paul gave an insight into how to cultivate that spirit in 2 Corinthians 4: "We having the same spirit of faith, according as it is written, I believed, and therefore have I spoken; we also believe, and therefore speak.... While we look not at the things which are seen, but at the things which are not seen: for the things which are seen are temporal; but the things which are not seen are eternal" (verses 13, 18).

The first and most fundamental fact these verses reveal about the spirit of faith is that it believes. What does it believe? The Word of God. What's more, faith believes God's Word just because God said it; whether natural circumstances seem to agree or not. Like so many people, I have been wondering how we can all heal once a new president is elected. With such a divided country, some people are going to be disappointed, frustrated, and perhaps disillusioned at a minimum. Others will be excited, hopeful, and ready to celebrate. How does a contemplative organization respond to the need for healing and reconciliation at such a time as this?

The Apostle Paul speaks of the hidden man of the heart. That is the YOU that is in you. The visible you are not the YOU that puts you over. It is the unseen YOU who wins the fight. The "seen you" may be very attractive or very repellent. It is the unseen YOU with whom we really wish to become acquainted. It is the unseen YOU, this hidden man of the heart, who runs the whole machinery, who is the boss of the institution. He is the man who is to build you into success. He is the fellow who raises the money to put you over. He is the one who made the "seen you" come across and make good. It is this unseen YOU to whom I am writing this morning. I am trying to reach him and cause him to make the "seen you" study, work, and make yourself worthwhile in life's game. It is the unseen YOU who makes the "seen you'" worthwhile and makes you do things that have commercial value, who makes you do things that the world is waiting to have done. I am saying to the unseen You, "Get behind this 'seen you'. Make him work. Make him study. Make him dig until he has won the fight."

I will call you "BOSS" throughout this book because I am convinced that by the time you finish reading this book you will become a boss on your own. My boss, believe in the sun even when it is not shining. Believe in love even when you don't feel it. Believe in God even when He is silent. Whatever you believe, with conviction, becomes your reality. You always act in a manner consistent with your deepest and most intensely held beliefs, whether they are true or not. And all your beliefs are learned. At one time, you did not have them. Your beliefs largely determine your reality. You do not believe what you *see*; you rather *see* what you already believe. You can have life-enhancing beliefs that make you happy and optimistic, or you can have negative beliefs about yourself and your potential that act as barricades to the realization of everything that is truly possible for you. The most destructive beliefs you can have are your *self-limiting beliefs*. These are beliefs about yourself and your potential that hold you back. Most of them are not true. Most of them are the result of information you have accepted without question, often from early childhood. Even if it is completely untrue, if you *believe* yourself to be limited in areas such as achieving wonderful health and happiness and earning a lot of money, that will become your truth.

Start to believe in you and your goals; It's timeless advice really. You've heard it a million times before, but this time you need to let it sink in. If you want to be successful, you have to believe in yourself. Believe in yourself. The future belongs to those who believe in the beauty of their dreams. Never feel guilty for doing what is best for yourself and others. Have faith and believe in your journey to success. Everything has to happen exactly as it did to get you to where you are going next. Believe in yourself because you are braver and bolder than you think, more talented than you know and capable of more than you can imagine. I believe in you, you can do it. This is your life, so you have to do what is right for you. Nobody else is walking in your shoes. If you want to live life on a new level you have to set your goals, see the vision, make the plans, and take daily consistent action. Consistency is the key, so many people want the good life but just give up after a few days or they don't even try. If you are truly serious about moving your life in a new direction you need to take action every single passing day.

Don't believe in yourself because it's your destiny to be successful. Don't believe in yourself because you've got a foolproof plan. Don't believe in yourself because you really want it. These are fairy tales spun to us, with no real serving purpose whatsoever. Believe in yourself because you know that you're going to put in the work. Believe in yourself because you know, as long you're still breathing by tomorrow, that you will continue to work towards where you want to be. Believe in yourself because you know you'll overcome the next hurdle you're presented with. Believe in yourself, you can achieve anything that you set your mind to. There are no limits out here, the only limits are those that you impose upon yourself. Dream, believe and take action. Identify what you truly want and how you truly want to live your life, and take action. Start to create the life of your dreams. Start small, dream big and don't ever give up.

Your beliefs brought you this far. And what you say reflects what you believe. Joel Osten said. *"poor mouth produces poor life."* Now is the time to change the direction of your mouth and your life will embrace a turn.

Arise and Make a Difference; the Drive Behind Success

Believe the people who tells you, 'you can do it' and ignore those saying 'you can't' Never allow your family, mentors, friends or whoever to tell you that you can't achieve your dreams.

You have to go after what you want or you will be confined to the life that you have stumbled into. The majority of people are confined to a life of mediocrity because they don't bother making a determined effort in the pursuit of what their heart yearns for, and they just live their whole lives like cowards, afraid to move out of their comfort zone, but it isn't really the comfort zone as people like to call it, it is the lazy zone, the just getting by zone, the cowardice zone, the conformist zone, the average zone, the mediocre zone, and the timid zone. You have to know that you have something within you, and that is greatness.

Within you is where the true growth occurs that will enable you to live the life of your dreams. The mind is the key that will unlock the door to your potential, your fearlessness, your courage, your ambition, your drive, your determination, your hunger, your grit, your perseverance, and your greatness. Do away with the mindset of mediocrity, you have to step up your game and take your life to a new level. The time is now to go after what you truly want, change your mentality and your life will start to change. We do not see the world as it is, but as we are. When you change for the better then everything around you will change for the better. Your outer world is a reflection of your inner world. If you do not believe that you can achieve anything that you set your mind to it is because you have some false internal beliefs about yourself. Your beliefs are what dictate how you live your life. If you don't believe that you can become successful then you will not take any action, and you will just continue doing the same mediocre things day after day, and you will never chase after your dreams.

Your calling is to believe in humanity as God believes in you. You are a resilient person. You are creative. You are relational. We need to believe in each other and we need each other to grow this country into what she can become. God has blessed this land and we are called to live into that blessing wherever we are. Belief in Something Better Is a Key to Success. Enough of the negative thinking and believe! Think positive and believe in yourself. Believe that you are a world changer. Refuse to accept the poor background of your family. No! the background of your family has nothing to do with your success tomorrow. Decide to make a change in the status of your family. Maybe you think you are the only one going through tough time but that is a fallacy. Hear me, I also have a poor background. I grew up from a poor family who barely ate three square meal daily. But this didn't eat me up, rather it generated in me the gratification to rise to the apex. Look I believe strongly in myself that I don't see the sky to be my limit but rather my beginning.

Many of us begin our leadership journey with negative thoughts and beliefs, such as: "I'm tired of living in debt"; "I'm sick of struggling say hard without the payoff," or "I'll never succeed; the odds against it are just too great." "When we begin to believe the never, the nothings, the no hopes, we have come to believe the great lie; that change cannot happen for us," says Mundahl. When we cease to believe, the body will find a way to stop as well. I couldn't agree more. Negative beliefs erode our very health and well-being. One of the ways for leaders to reclaim their authentic self and power, according to Steve Mundahl, a proponent of positive thinking, is to realize that "every negative thought also can contain the seeds for change." He reminds us that in nature, a problem (poison ivy) often exists right next to the solution (jewelweed). In the case of the above, I'm tired of living in debt becomes "Then I will find a better way." I'm sick of struggling so hard without the payoff becomes "I will learn from this experience." And I'll never succeed becomes "If I keep at it, something is going to work." His idea is that "believing is the key component to change. It takes really wanting to change," says Mundahl.

Believe You Deserve It! Believe you deserve that opportunity! Many of us struggle with low self-esteem and at a core level, we don't feel we deserve success and abundance. Guess what? If you don't believe you deserve it, you will resist it when it arrives. You may do this unconsciously by sabotaging your own efforts, or we may outright refuse to even try. We must first understand and then truly believe that we do deserve success and abundance. In addition, we must be willing to receive it. We're so good at giving to others, but many of us won't accept help or blessings for ourselves. We feel it is better to give than to receive, and in some ways it is. However, that doesn't mean we shouldn't receive at all. Be willing to believe that you deserve to be successful and happy. Then be willing to accept that abundance when it arrives. Affirm aloud to the universe each day, "I joyfully accept all of the abundance and happiness the universe has for me, now."

Let us consider the power of belief, as it is now being established, by a man who is well known to all of civilization, Mahatma Gandhi, of India. In this man the world has one of the most astounding examples known to civilization, of the possibilities of belief. Gandhi wields more potential power than any man living at this time, and this, despite the fact that he has none of the orthodox tools of power, such as money, battle ships, soldiers, and materials of warfare. Gandhi has no money, he has no home, he does not own a suit of clothes, but he does have power. How does he come by that power? He created it out of his understanding of the principle of faith, and through his ability to transplant that faith into the minds of two hundred million people. Gandhi has accomplished, through the influence of belief, that which the strongest military power on earth could not, and never will accomplish through soldiers and military equipment. He has accomplished the astounding feat of influencing two hundred million minds to amalgamate and move in unison, as a single mind. There are no limitations to the mind except those we acknowledge both poverty and riches are the offspring of thought.

The starting point of unlocking your potential, and accomplishing more than you ever have before, is for you to *challenge* your self-limiting beliefs. You begin this process of freeing yourself from self-limiting beliefs by imagining that, whatever they are, they are completely untrue. Imagine for the moment that you have no limitations on your abilities at all. Imagine that you could be, do, or have anything you really wanted in life. Imagine that your potential is unlimited in any way. For example, envisage that you could be earning twice as much as you are earning today. Envision that you could be living in a bigger house, driving a better car, and enjoying a more expensive lifestyle. Imagine that you have the ability to be one of the top people in your field. Envisage that you are one of the most popular, powerful, and persuasive personalities in your social and business world. Imagine that you are calm, confident, and unafraid of anything. Imagine that you could set and achieve any goal you put your mind to. This is how you begin changing your thinking and changing your life. The preliminary point of eliminating your fears, and releasing your potential, is to reprogram your mental hard drive with new, positive, constructive, and courageous beliefs about yourself and your future.

It is not what happens to you in life that is important. It is only *how you react* to what happens. It doesn't matter where you're coming from, either. All that really matters is where you are going. And where you are going is limited only by your own imagination. And since your imagination is unlimited, your future is unlimited as well. *These* are the basic premises and beliefs you need to fulfill your potential. Remember, whatever you believe, with feeling, becomes your reality. The greater the intensity of your belief, the more emotion you combine with it, the greater the impact it has on your behavior and on everything that happens to you. If you absolutely believe that you are destined to be a great success, and you hold to this belief no matter what happens, then there is nothing in the world that can stop you from becoming that great success.

If you absolutely believe that you are a good person with tremendous abilities and that you are going to do remarkable things with your life, that belief will express itself through all of your actions and will eventually become your reality. The biggest responsibility you have to yourself is to change your beliefs on the inside so that they are consistent with the realities you wish to enjoy on the outside. You can always tell what your beliefs really are by looking at what you do. You always express your true values in your actions. You always act on the outside consistent with who you really are, and what you really believe, on the inside. One of the best ways to determine your true beliefs is to think about how you behave when you are angry, upset, or under pressure of any kind. This is when they come out. As

Terrance wrote, *"Circumstances do not make the man; they only reveal him to himself."* (And to others!). By using the Law of Reversibility, you can develop within yourself the values, beliefs, and qualities you most admire by acting as if you already had them, whenever they are called for by the circumstances of your life. To develop courage, force yourself to act courageously, even when you are afraid. To develop integrity, speak and act with complete honesty, even if you feel like shading the truth or cutting corners. Soon your beliefs will mirror your acts, and your acts will mirror your beliefs.

CHAPTER TWO

THE KEY OF DISCIPLINE

"Mental toughness is many things and rather difficult to explain. Its qualities are sacrifice and self-denial. Also, most importantly, it is combined with a perfectly disciplined will that refuses to give in. It's a state of mind - - you could call it character in action."

(Vince Lombardi)

Discipline is a concept everyone is aware of, but few truly understand. The most successful people in life exert discipline on a daily basis. It is vital to every living being and without it, the world around us would be chaos. To be a great and inspiring leader, you must constantly display restraint. Not giving into something you truly want is a sign of strength. Making the right decisions in life can make or break you, and this type of person tends to make the right decisions. Regardless of where you exert this self-restraint, it will help to promote achievement in your life.

Talent without discipline is like an octopus on roller skates. There's plenty of movement, but you never know if it's going to be forward, backwards, or sideways. Discipline brings stability and structure into your life. It teaches you to be responsible and respectful. The observance of well-defined rules is the basis of society. If there were no discipline, people would do whatever they wanted and make mistakes without putting the consideration of others first and foremost. It promotes good human behavior to better society and make it a more enjoyable place for everyone to live.

The ability for an individual to have self-restraint allows them to behave in a consistently stringent and controlled manner. A lack of this ability can have disastrous results. Do you think a company is going to tolerate a person who is consistently late to work or who procrastinates in doing their work? It is evident how these behaviors will weaken the image of a business.

Think of sports: discipline is the fundamental aspect on which sports have been created. Every player must adhere to the rules of the game. This is why umpires and referees exist. Whoever does not follow these guidelines will be penalized for violating the rules of the sport. Persons in high authority must demonstrate high levels of restraint constantly; they cannot just speak however they see fit. A smart leader knows when to hold his tongue and when to speak. Discipline helps to train your mind and character, building a sense of self-control and the practice of obedience. Self-discipline is a form of freedom. Freedom from laziness and lethargy, freedom from the expectations and demands of others, freedom from weakness and fear and doubt. Self-discipline allows a pitcher to feel his individuality, his inner strength, his talent. He is master of, rather than a slave to, his thoughts and emotions.

There are two types of discipline: internal and external. Internal discipline is your self-restraint and your ability to differentiate right from wrong. External discipline is according to societal norms, such as following the law. It is not sufficient enough to possess great qualities; we need the ability to manage them. Too many people are susceptible to instant gratification. People lacking control are unable to look at the long-term effects of their actions. This further demonstrates why this is such a crucial skill to have in life, especially if you must make a difference. It is probably the most crucial factor when trying to achieve a goal. It allows you to choose from different options and by following these options you can garner the success you sought out for. It additionally gives you the authority to overcome any obstacles that come your way. Discipline is the bridge between goals and accomplishment.

This ability can be developed or strengthened at any given time if you put your mind to it. Make promises and make sure you deliver. Make the genuine effort to align your actions and behaviors with your thoughts. Exercise; get your mind and body into shape. Resist the urge to give into negative behaviors, instead focus on all of the positive attributes. The foundational attribute all successful people share is self-discipline. It is their self-discipline that allows them to keep the commitments that they make to themselves. Successful people know that their good intentions don't add up to a hill of beans. It's their actions that make a difference in their results. You've heard it before, but it bears repeating: successful people do what unsuccessful people aren't willing to do. Listen! it's not that the unsuccessful are unable. They are just unwilling. You might have a dream of becoming a business man. Every business has a client or customer to transact business with. Your dream clients already have a supplier. Maybe even a partner.

Ignoring and neglecting your dream clients doesn't do anything to move you closer to the relationships that you need. The discipline of nurturing is what eventually opens the relationships that open opportunities. Your effort to create value for your dream clients before claiming any is what will eventually bear fruit. But only if you exercise the self-discipline to create and share new ideas with your dream clients. Who you are as a professional salesperson is visible in your clients' list. Your clients and dream clients are judging you. They are watching to see if you keep your commitments. This is as true for your commitments great or small.

Charles Murray once said; "*Until one is committed, there is hesitancy, the chance to draw back, always ineffectiveness. Concerning all acts of initiative and creation, there is an elementary truth, the ignorance of which kills countless ideas and splendid plans; that the moment that one definitely commits oneself, then providence moves too. All sorts of things occur to help one that would never otherwise have occurred. A whole stream of events issues from the decision, raising in one's favor all manner of unforeseen incidences and meetings and material assistance that no man could have dreamed would have come his way."* The discipline of following up is more than just sending the email you promised to send. It's also the discipline of doing high quality follow-up work. You make it easier for your client to say "yes" when you observe the discipline of follow-up, keeping your word and doing quality work.

Practice the discipline of follow up and be someone who can always be counted on. You can't afford to rest on your laurels. You did the work to turn your dream client into a paying client, but becoming complacent can cost you their business. From quarter to quarter, you have to improve what you do for your clients. You have to share with them the value that you are creating, as well as your plans for creating even more value together in the future. Practice the discipline of improvement and bring clients ideas that help to create new value. The environment that we live and sell in is like nothing we've ever seen. The forces of globalization, commoditization, and disintermediation make for some tough sledding. Success means that you have to become the very best possible version of yourself. You need to become.

The self-discipline of personal development begins with your ability to eliminate distractions. Instead of filling down time with distractions and novelties, you have to use some of that time to improve yourself through reading, studying, taking a class, or attending action-oriented webinars. You have to invest both time and money in improving the only real asset you will ever have: You! Practice the discipline of personal development and continue to grow so you can make a greater contribution. Can I ask you a question? What is that unseen, unknown quality that is the difference between those who dream and those who do not? Discipline. Yes! Work all the time you work. Discipline yourself to keep yourself focused on the most valuable use of your time. Don't allow other people to put you "off your game." When you have coffee breaks or lunches, have them when they best suit you, not when they best suit the clock.

Educational institutions speak of disciplines, or branches of instruction. Yet few of the students that pass through those halls ever learn the power and joy of a truly disciplined life. Discipline is more than education. It is at the heart of good business. It is the secret of successful athletes. It is the key to great men. Most of all, it is at the heart of what is meant by being a true follower of Jesus Christ. it is interesting that the word discipline comes from the same word for disciple. Discipline is indeed hard to define. It is best understood by its absence. When there is a lack of discipline, it always shows. The subject of discipline is not just for college students; it is for all of us, especially you. It is not just a matter for youth; it is for life.

Hear me, the man who cannot control himself can never control others. Self-control sets a mighty example for one's followers, which the more intelligent will emulate. Discipline comes through self-control. This means that one must control all negative qualities. Before you can control conditions, you must first control yourself. Self-mastery is the hardest job you will ever tackle. If you do not conquer self, you will be conquered by self. You may see at the same time both your best friend and your greatest enemy, simply by stepping in front of a mirror.

If you cannot get control of yourself, do not try to get rich. It makes no sense to invest, make money, and blow it. It is the lack of self-discipline that causes most lottery winners to go broke soon after winning millions. It is the lack of self-discipline that causes people who get a raise to immediately go out and buy a new car or take a cruise.

CHAPTER THREE

THE KEY OF DETEMINATION AND PERSEVERANCE

"As long as we are persistence in our pursuit of our deepest destiny, we will continue to grow."

Denis Waitley

Determination and Perseverance is another key to making a difference. Everyone deep down in their heart has their own passion or an immortal flame that cannot be diminished. But often, we forgotten how to express the fire that buried deeply inside of us and worst, too ashamed to reveal and share the true self of us. Do you want to know the reasons such people have? I am too shy. No one will appreciate and understand my passions. It's a complete waste of time, it's all just wasted efforts. If you fall in that category of people then ***you need to stop!***

Scripture says *a little sleep or slumber and poverty will knock on your door…* Refuse to be a lazy bone. Stop sleeping and shine your eyes to the point where you become restless until you attain that dream.

You must also know that there is no such thing as ***something for nothing!*** The secret to success cannot be gotten without a price, although the price is far less than its value. You cannot have it at any price if you are not intentionally searching for it. It cannot be given away; it cannot be purchased for money. If you are ready for it, it is available to you. The secret serves equally well, all who are ready for it. Understand that riches are not beyond your reach, that you can still be what you wish to be. Money, fame, recognition and happiness can be had by all who are ready and determined to have these blessings

When you first toward a goal, filled with and You must feel just know that accomplish begin work you must be passion, fire excitement. invincible and you can whatever you

> **"Sometimes we stumble on greatness but lack of persistence makes us walk away from it."**

desire. Take off running toward your goal, determined to make it happen, and you can make it happen. You may struggle through a few of them, but then making excuses for not working on your goals won't help you. What is your reason for wanting a particular goal? Let's say your goal is to buy a house. Ask yourself why you want that. Your answer may be something along the lines of, "Because I want to own my own property rather than paying rent for the rest of my life." Okay good. But why? What does it matter if you own your own property or pay rent? Your answer might now be, "Because I want to have the house paid off by the time I retire, so I don't have to worry about paying rent or a mortgage payment on a fixed income." Bravo! But why? What will that do for you? Keep asking yourself why? and writing down your answers until you get to the "meat" of your desire. Once you have a clear desire in mind you are not far from success. Let me say it again. If your goal is to buy a house, you likely have a lot of smaller goals that must be accomplished first. You will need to build up a savings for the down payment. You may need to clean up your credit report and pay down existing debt. You will need to see if you qualify for a mortgage loan. Always keep your ultimate goal in mind, but focus on the smaller steps that will get you there first. If I wanted to drive to a particular destination, I would have to pay attention to the route I need to take to get there, not just the destination.

Resolve in advance that you will never quit once you have started toward your goal. No matter how many setbacks or obstacles you experience, make the decision that you will keep on picking yourself up and persisting until you eventually succeed. By deciding in advance that you will persist, no matter what the difficulty, you give yourself a psychological edge. When the difficulties do arise, you will be mentally prepared to plow through them rather than quitting. Your willingness and ability to persist are what will eventually guarantee your success.

Without perseverance, you will be defeated, even before you start. With perseverance you will win. If you have ever experienced a nightmare, you will realize the value of perseverance. You are lying in bed, half awake, with a feeling that you are about to smother. You are unable to turn over, or to move a muscle. You realize that you must begin to regain control over your muscles. Through determined effort of will-power, you finally manage to move the fingers of one hand. By continuing to move your fingers, you extend your control to the muscles of one arm, until you can lift it. Then you gain control of the other arm in the same manner. You finally gain control over the muscles of one leg, and then extend it to the other leg. Then; with one supreme effort of will; you regain complete control over your muscular system, and "snap" out of your nightmare. The trick has been turned step by step.

You may find it necessary to "snap" out of your mental inertia through a similar procedure, moving slowly at first, then increasing your speed, until you gain complete control over your will. Be persistent no matter how slowly you may, at first, have to move. with persistence and determination will come success. If you select your "Master Mind" group with care, you will have in it at least one person who will aid you in the development of perseverance. Some men who have amassed great fortunes did so because of necessity. They developed the habit of perseverance and determination, because they were so closely driven by circumstances, that they had to become persistent. There is no substitute for perseverance! It cannot be replaced by any other quality! Remember this, and it will hearten you in the beginning, when the going may seem difficult and slow.

Those who have cultivated the habit of perseverance and determination seem to enjoy insurance against failure. No matter how many times they are defeated, they finally arrive at the top of the ladder. Sometimes it appears that there is a hidden Guide whose duty is to test men through all sorts of discouraging experiences. Those who pick themselves up after defeat and keep on trying, arrive; the world cries, "Bravo! I knew you could do it!" The hidden Guide lets no one enjoy great achievement without passing the perseverance test. Those who can't take it, simply do not make the grade. Those who can "take it" are bountifully rewarded for their perseverance and determination. They receive, as their compensation, whatever goal they are pursuing. That is not all! They receive something infinitely more important than material compensation; the knowledge that *"every failure brings with it the seed of an equivalent advantage."*

Know what you want, and have the determination to by that desire until you realize it. Don't say, "if things were different, I would do something." Do something with them as they are. Facing your life as it is now and winning is the object. When things go hard and money stops coming in, or you lose your job and everything goes wrong, take account of stock. See what is wrong. See what you have forgotten, and go on and conquer. We dream what we would do if ... Now wipe out the "if." Dream, and do it regardless of circumstances. You say, "That cannot be done." It can be done. There is no "can't" about it. The man who wills to do it, who puts up the fight, and is willing to do the work, can put it over.

A young man discovered a strain cover with gold high up in the foothill. He needed power. He needed money. He needed to know how to develop it. He struggled and worked and failed. Sitting down one night after a long hard day, tired, clear through and through, he said to himself, "I know where my difficulty is. I don't know anything about this rock. I don't know anything about Geology and I know nothing about mining. I am going down to the city and find out." He came down to the city and went to the head of the mining department in the college, and laid the case before him. The professor called up a mining engineer. He met the young man. The young man told his story. The engineer said that he must go and see the strain. It took about a week to get there. After the engineer had seen it, he said, "There are millions there. But it will cost a great deal to get in here and to develop it. You will have to organize a stock company or sell it. Which will you do?" The young man said, "I am going to develop it." It took him a year of hard training and study.

He gave himself utterly to it. Through the long winter months, he drove himself until, when the springtime came, he had acquired the knowledge that he needed. It made him millions. The trouble with too many people is that they want to get it too easily. Most of us say, "If I had had a chance; but circumstances were against me. I don't have an education. I didn't have the jerk." We lay our failure to the lack of opportunity. The other fellow, handicapped worse than we, made opportunities. He fought until opportunities came to him.

Success belongs to the man who simply wills to do it. He is the man who makes success come his way.

The fellow who lies down and says, "I can't do it," is a failure. Never lose heart because the first efforts fail. Go back and find the reason. Pick up the wreckage of old failures and build them into success. You can do it. It's all about having the determination to push harder no matter the storms that come your way. A church member once asked me this question; "Is it good to have a bad beginning?" My answer was a simple "NO". He asked this question because he always start badly academically but have a good end and therefore, he thinks it is good. I further told him that the fact that you always start badly and ends good that not mean you were born to always starts badly. You were born to start on a good note. In this world the results that we obtain at any level of our lives is influenced by the environment and current circumstances around us. Not all environments will permit a 'good' end for a 'bad' beginning. After all, superlatively 'best' is the greatest of 'good' and 'better' so why yearn for 'good' when 'best' is the greatest. Therefore, desire to always start on a 'good' not so that you can obtain the 'best' result. Be determined to start well and persevere to the end. Most of us are good "starters" but poor "finishers" of everything we begin. Moreover, people are prone to give up at the first signs of defeat. There is no substitute for persistence.

The person who makes persistence his watch-word, discovers that "Old Man Failure" finally becomes tired, and makes his departure. Failure cannot cope with persistence. The majority of people are ready to throw their aims and purposes overboard, and give up at the first sign of opposition or misfortune. A few carry on despite all opposition, until they attain their goal. You're only poor if you give up. The most important thing is that you did something. Most people only talk and dream of getting rich.

Write out a list of the smaller steps that will help you reach your goal, and then begin working on them one at a time. Don't overwhelm yourself by thinking only of that big, shining vision of the completed project. No matter what obstacles come up, no matter if your desire and determination begin to fade. True success comes to those who just won't give up. Make a promise to yourself that you will continue working toward your goals no matter what happens. Write this promise out and put it somewhere you will see it. Read it aloud to yourself every single day. Keep reminding yourself that nothing will change unless you change it. Fuel your determination with positive thoughts and keep moving forward. If obstacles come up, find a way around them. If there is absolutely no way around a particular obstacle, switch your focus and begin working on another aspect of your goals. Many times, obstacles will fade away if given enough time, or sometimes a solution presents itself when we least expect it. Let your determination glow hot and bright, and burn away all doubts and fears.

Know that you can do it, and you will. Your positive affirmations help you to create a stronger sense of self-love and self-confidence, increase your abundance and prosperity, discover your life purpose, attract great opportunities, develop healthy relationships, foster healing and well-being, maintain a healthy weight and body image, and attain greater inner peace and calm. The MP3 meditation takes all of these great affirmations and sets them to music, creating a soothing meditation you will want to listen to again and again. Nothing in the world, can take the place of perseverance and determination. Talent will not; nothing is more common, than unsuccessful people with talent. Genius will not; un rewarded genius is almost a proverb. Education will not; the world is full of educated derelicts. perseverance and determination alone, are almost omnipotent. Now I'm not saying you should not get an education, but you can have an education, and be weak inside, and never experience the opportunity that education could have provided for you, because you just didn't have the perseverance and determination to make it happen.

The Apostle Peter (in 2 Peter 1:5), gives a list of qualities, that you have to "Add" to your faith, if you are going to be a success. Some of these qualities, could be captured as "perseverance and determination". You have to persevere: It does not matter how many times you are turned down. If you are trying to get a qualification or pass an exam, don't quit just because you failed; try again, and again, and again! If you are trying to get a job, don't quit because you got a rejection. If you are trying to build your career, don't quit because some guy at work shouted at you!

If you are trying to build a business, don't quit simply because the business climate is bad, in your community. Or, because someone let you down. Or, because your government did not do something for you. Maybe you lost your job, and you have been looking, and looking and looking. Don't give up! You might have even gone bankrupt. Start again. Don't quit! You have to be determined.

A good boxer knows, that being knocked down does not mean you are out; you get up, and carry on fighting, with even greater determination. Every opportunity that you will pursue, if it is good, will invariably draw opposition. Imagine an eagle in a storm, its "mounts" the winds, like someone climbing a staircase. Such is the metaphor of becoming successful. Always anticipate opposition, and learn to mount it, to take you even higher, in the pursuit of your goals.

I was enticed by a story from info@wealthygreeks.com. A man was caught by the "gold fever" in the gold-rush days, and went west to dig and grow rich. He had never heard that more gold has been mined from the brains of men than has ever been taken from the earth. He staked a claim and went to work with pick and shovel. The going was hard, but his lust for gold was definite. After weeks of labor, he was rewarded by the discovery of the shining ore. He needed machinery to bring the ore to the surface. Quietly, he covered up the mine, retraced his footsteps to his home, told his relatives and a few neighbors of the "strike." They got together money for the needed machinery, and had it shipped. He and the family went back to work the mine. The first car of ore was mined, and shipped to a smelter.

The returns proved that they had one of the richest mines in Colorado! A few more cars of that ore would clear the debts. Then would come the big killing in profits. Down went the drills! Up went the hopes of this man and his group! Then something happened! The vein of gold ore disappeared! They had come to the end of the rainbow, and the pot of gold was no longer there! They drilled on, desperately trying to pick up the vein again all to no avail. Finally, they decided to **quit**. They sold the machinery to a junk man for a few hundred dollars, and took the train back home. Some "junk" men are dumb, but not this one! He called in a mining engineer to look at the mine and do a little calculating. The engineer advised that the project had failed because the owners were not familiar with "fault lines." His calculations showed that the vein would be found **just three feet from where the he had stopped drilling!** That is exactly where it was found! The "Junk" man took millions of dollars in ore from the mine, because he knew enough to seek expert counsel before giving up. For many of the most successful men this country has ever known, their greatest success came just one step beyond the point at which defeat had overtaken them. Failure is a trickster with a keen sense of irony and cunning. It takes great delight in tripping one when success is almost within reach

CHAPTER FOUR

THE KEY OF INTEGRITY

"Too many people overvalue what they are not and undervalue what they are." -- Malcolm Forbes

Congratulations! Welcome to the key of integrity. I chose to define integrity as the quality of being honest and having strong moral principles, or moral uprightness. It is a personal choice to hold one's self to consistent standards. In ethics, integrity is regarded as the honesty and truthfulness or accuracy of one's actions. Integrity can stand in opposition to hypocrisy, in that judging with the standards of integrity involves regarding internal consistency as a virtue, and suggests that parties holding within themselves apparently conflicting values should account for the discrepancy or alter their beliefs.

The word *integrity* evolved from the Latin adjective *integer*, meaning *whole* or *complete*. In other words integrity is the inner sense of "wholeness" deriving from qualities such as honesty and consistency of character. As such, one may judge that others "have integrity" to the extent that they act according to the values, beliefs and principles they claim to hold. Those who succeed are those that understand that life is about solving problems. They seek out the problems and develop the ability to solve them. The ability to move something forward when something bad happens. Before I continue to tell you more of integrity, I am obliged to ask you this simple but thoughtful question; Do You Have Integrity?

Think about it. Reflect on it and jot down your answer. Deep inside you is this great ability to operate in reality and deal with it. You possess in you not the desire to maintain but a real desire to grow and increase. Come on! Declare with me! "I Have the Ability to Increase and Grow"! Desire to change my dear. Change is difficult to implement but be bold and make the decision to change now! Growth won't happen because you feel you ought to do this. "Ought "is not a good motivator. So how do you change? You change when you play the **"movie,"** which is to take a hard reality look at your life and work, then play that reality forward to see if you like the way the future movie of your life and career plays out. In that way, you begin to experience the future losses, rewards, and consequences right now and get with reality.

When you look, for example, at your present performance, and the things that you are not getting, and then you realize that if you continue to do the same things expecting different results, you will *never get what you want*, you will change. If I could tell you only one value to live by, it would be integrity. success will come and go, but integrity is forever. Integrity means doing the right thing at all times and in all circumstances, whether or not anyone is watching. It takes having the courage to do the right thing, no matter what the consequences will be. Building a reputation of integrity takes years, but it takes only a second to lose, so never allow yourself to ever do anything that would damage your integrity. We live in a world where integrity isn't talked about nearly enough.

We live in a world where "the end justifies the means" has become an acceptable school of thought for far too many.

Sales people overpromise and under deliver, all in the name of making their quota for the month. Applicants exaggerate in job interviews because they desperately need a job. Directors overstate their projected earnings because they don't want the board of directors to replace them. Entrepreneurs overstate their pro formats because they want the highest valuation possible from an investor. Investors understate a company's value in order to negotiate a lower valuation in a deal. Customer service representatives cover up a mistake they made because they are afraid the client will leave them. Employees call in "sick" because they don't have any more paid time off when they actually just need to get their Christmas shopping done. The list could go on and on, and in each case the person committing the act of dishonesty told themselves they had a perfectly valid reason why the end result justified their lack of integrity.

Maybe you might have forgotten the tittle of the book you are reading so let me be kind to remind you again. *Arise and Make a Difference; The Drive Behind Success.* Believe you me just possessing the key of integrity is a step to climbing the ladder of making a difference. It may seem like people can gain power quickly and easily if they are willing to cut corners and act without the constraints of morality. Dishonesty may provide instant gratification in the moment but it will never last. I can think of several examples of people without integrity who are successful and who won without ever getting caught, which created a false perception of the path to success that one should follow. After all, each of these people could have gained the result they wanted in the moment, but unfortunately, that momentary result comes at an incredibly high price with far reaching consequences. That person has lost his or her ability to be trusted as a person of integrity, which is the most valuable quality anyone can have in his life.

Profit in dollars or power is temporary, but profit in a network of people who trust you as a person of integrity is forever. Every one person who trusts you will spread the word of that trust to at least a few of their associates, and word of your character will spread like wildfire. The value of the trust others has in you is far beyond anything that can be measured. For entrepreneurs it means investors that are willing to trust them with their money. For employees it means a manager or a boss that is willing to trust them with additional responsibility and growth opportunities. For companies it means customers that trust giving them more and more business. For you it means having an army of people that are willing to go the extra mile to help you because they know that recommending you to others will never bring damage to their own reputation of integrity. Yes! The value of the trust others has in you goes beyond anything that can be measured because it brings along with its limitless opportunities and endless possibilities. Contrast that with the person who cannot be trusted as a person of integrity.

Warren Buffet, Chairman and CEO of Berkshire Hathaway said it best: "In looking for people to hire, look for three qualities: integrity, intelligence, and energy. And if they don't have the first one, the other two will kill you." A person's dishonesty will eventually catch up to them. It may not be today, and it may not be for many years, but you can rest assured that at some point there will always be a reckoning. A word of advice to those who are striving for a reputation of integrity: Avoid those who are not trustworthy. Do not do business with them. Do not associate with them. Do not make excuses for them. Do not allow yourself to get enticed into believing that "while they may be dishonest with others, they would never be dishonest with me." If someone is dishonest in any aspect of his life you can be guaranteed that he will be dishonest in many aspects of his life.

You cannot dismiss even those little acts of dishonesty, such as the person who takes two newspapers from the stand when they paid for only one. After all, if a person cannot be trusted in the simplest matters of honesty then how can they possibly be trusted to uphold lengthy and complex business contracts? It is important to realize that others pay attention to those you have chosen to associate with, and they will inevitably judge your character by the character of your friends. Why is that? It is best explained by this quote; "When you lie down with dogs you get fleas." Inevitably we become more and more like the people we surround ourselves with day to day. If we surround ourselves with people who are dishonest and willing to cut corners to get ahead, then we'll surely find ourselves following a pattern of first enduring their behavior, then accepting their behavior, and finally adopting their behavior. If you want to build a reputation as a person of integrity then surround yourself with people of integrity. You can be sure of making a great difference with this advice.

Anytime I pass by the University Junior high school at the University of Cape Coast, I always read their motto that is boldly inscribed on their building; *"Love Good and Hate Evil"*. This ultimately reminds any reader of the integrity of the school. What can readers read about your life? Integrity or dishonesty? I want to borrow the words of God when He spoke to the Israelites. God said *"I presents to you this day life and death; but I advise you to choose life."* This very minute I also present to you, integrity and dishonest to choose one. But of course, I will advise you to choose integrity because it will drive you to the ultimate destination of making a difference.

If you ask company executives to reveal their "core values," integrity is always one of their first answers, says Joel C. Peterson, chairman of the board of JetBlue Airways and a Stanford University professor of management. The single most important ingredient to business success is trust, and trust starts with integrity. Think of a bridge or a structure with integrity; they're all bolted together in a way that can withstand shocks. Talk to the people around you to get a handle on your integrity, recommends Tony Simons, author of *"The Integrity Dividend: Leading by the Power of Your Word"*. Find ways to get honest feedback from others. You need to find out if and that goes double if you're a boss you have the appropriate level of trust. Integrity stands as a driver of trust." I will advise you to let those around you call you out…. Be willing to have people police you.

Your trusted advisers should be people who will tell you whether you're acting with integrity or whether there's a better way to handle something." To be sure that you are possessing the key of integrity fulfill your promises. If you break a promise, you must apologize, but don't let this become a pattern; keep appointments. Doing so affects you professionally and personally (practicing your faith, staying fit, being present for family, etc.); Before you make a commitment. Stop and soberly reflect on whether you are 100 percent sure you can deliver. You need to be dispassionate in that evaluation. Get comfortable with saying 'no'. No one can say yes to everything and follow through on it all; Examine how you react in knee-jerk situations. As well as how you make longer-term commitments (e.g., attending events, completing projects, etc.). Use this introspection to become self-aware, keep score and improve; Polish your communication skills. Re-read that email or report before you send it; plan what you will say in oral presentations, seminars, symposiums, conferences and phone calls. Ambiguous communication leads to broken promises. Ask someone to proof-read written communications and point out ambiguities before you distribute them.

Consider the habits and skills you need to develop to enhance your integrity. You might need to stop certain actions (e.g., speaking impulsively or sugarcoating your responses). And you might need to improve on others: building your personal courage because fear holds you back from acting with integrity. Issue apologies faster, simpler and aimed more at containing the damage you may have done than at justifying yourself. Avoid people who lack integrity. Do not do business with them. Do not associate with them. Do not make excuses for them. It's important to realize that others pay attention to those you have chosen to associate with, and they will unavoidably critic your character by the character of your friends.

Most of us have heard the saying, "You are what you eat." I have a different slant. I say, "You become what you study." In other words, be vigilant what you learn, because your mind is so powerful that you become what you put in your head. For example, if you study driving, you then tend to drive. If you don't want to be a driver anymore, then you need to study something else. When it comes to money, the masses generally have one basic method they learned in school and it's this: Work for money. The predominant method I see in the world is that every day lots of people get up, go to work, earn money, pay bills, balance checkbooks, buy some mutual funds, and go back to work. That is the basic method, or recipe. If you're tired of what you're doing, or you're not making enough, it's simply a case of changing the formula via which you make money. All I am saying in this chapter is that be moved and influenced by integrity and will be assured of making a huge difference in life.

Making a difference in life and becoming successful does not begin with your peripheral systems. It begins from your mind. The next chapter will therefore tell you how important the mind is in making a difference.

CHAPTER FIVE

THE MIND AS THE ORIGINATOR OF SUCCESS

Thought is the original source of all wealth, all success, all material gain, all great discoveries and inventions, and of all achievement.

Claude M. Bristol

Hello my boss, you are welcome to an exciting part of this book. The mind as the originator of making a difference and becoming successful. It's very imperative to begin this session with one of my personal quotes; *"What you let into your minds shapes the state of your soul"*. The central purpose of this topic is to help you change your thinking in such a way that you become absolutely unstoppable in achieving any goal you can set for yourself.

The Law of Correspondence says that your outer world is a mirror of your inner world. It says in the Bible, *"As a man thinketh in his heart, so is he."* This means that as you see yourself and think about yourself in your conscious mind, your perception of the outer world changes and conforms to fit a picture consistent with it. This is the central message of this book. The most influential factors in your thinking and feeling will almost always be the other people in your life. Successful people are those who form the habit of associating with other positive, success-oriented people. Unsuccessful people, by default, end up associating with people who are not going anywhere with their lives. Both sets of people become more and more like the people with whom they most identify.

Your goal is to develop yourself to the point expressively where you become like an irresistible force of nature. You will be like the tide coming in, or like a powerful storm that sweeps across the land. Your aim is to become so confident, courageous, strong, and resolute that you can set any goal for yourself with the firm knowledge that you can learn what you need to learn, and do what you need to do, to eventually achieve it. You will become so persistent and determined that nothing and no one can slow you down or alter your course. You will become truly unstoppable!

The way you think and feel about yourself, including your beliefs and expectations about what is possible for you, determines everything you do and everything that happens to you. When you change the quality of your thinking, you change the quality of your life, sometimes instantly. When you begin to change your thinking about your goals and possibilities, your beliefs and actions will change. You will find yourself doing more and more of the things you need to do to make your dreams come true. You will continually expect good things to happen to you, and you will seldom be disappointed. You will begin attracting all kinds of wonderful people and opportunities into your life. Your whole world will begin to correspond, on the outside, with the wonderful goals and pictures that you are creating on the inside.

You become what you perceive yourself to be. The perceptions you create about yourself will go a long way to determine who you become in life. If you see yourself to be a failure in life so shall it be about you. In the same vain if you see yourself to be a success so shall it be. Your perception will determine your progression in life. Perhaps the most important mental and spiritual principle ever discovered is that you become what you think about most of the time. Your outer world is very much a mirror image of your inner world. What is going on outside of you is a reflection of what is going in inside of you. You can tell the inner condition of a person by looking at the outer conditions of his or her life. And it cannot be otherwise.

> *"whatever the mind of man can conceive and believe it can achieve"*
>
> Napoleon Hill

Your mind is extraordinarily powerful. Your thoughts control and determine almost everything that happens to you. They can raise or lower your heart rate, improve or interfere with your digestion, change the chemical composition of your blood, and help you to sleep or keep you awake at night. Your thoughts can make you happy or sad, sometimes in an instant. They can make you alert and aware, or distracted and depressed. They can make you popular or unpopular, confident or insecure, positive or negative. Your thoughts can make you feel powerful or powerless, a victim or a victor, a hero or a coward. In your physical life, your thoughts can make you a success or a failure, prosperous or poverty-stricken, respected or ignored. Your thoughts, and the actions that they trigger, determine your whole life. And the best news of all is that they are completely under your own control

Every man is what he is because of the dominating thoughts which he permits to occupy his mind. Thoughts that a man deliberately places in his own mind, and encourages with sympathy, and with which he mixes any one or more of the emotions, constitute the motivating forces which direct and control his every movement, act, and deed! Successful people are those who think more effectively than unsuccessful people. They approach their lives, relationships, goals, problems, and experiences differently from others. They sow better seeds, and as a result they reap better lives. If you learn to think and act like other successful, happy, healthy, and prosperous people, you will soon enjoy the kind of lives they do. When you change your thinking, you change your life.

Thoughts which are mixed with any of the feelings of emotions, constitute a "magnetic" force which attracts, from the vibrations of the universe, other similar, or related thoughts. A thought thus "magnetized" with emotion may be compared to a seed which, when planted in fertile soil, germinates, grows, and multiplies itself over and over again, until that which was originally one small seed, becomes countless millions of seeds of the same brand. The ether is a great cosmic mass of eternal forces of vibration. It is made up of both destructive vibrations and constructive vibrations. It carries, at all times, vibrations of fear, poverty, disease, failure, misery; and vibrations of prosperity, health, success, and happiness. From the great storehouse of the universe, the human mind is constantly attracting vibrations which harmonize with that which dominates the human mind. Any thought, idea, plan, or purpose which one holds in one's mind attracts, from the vibrations of the Universe, a host of its relatives, adds these "relatives" to its own force, and grows until it becomes the dominating, motivating master of the individual in whose mind it has been housed.

Way too many people have already decided that a job is a way to pay the bills and nothing more. They reached that conclusion after beating their head against the wall trying to get more out of a job than just a paycheck, to no avail. There is only one thing over which you have complete control, and that is the content of your own mind. Only you can decide what you are going to think, and how you are going to think about it. This power, this control, is all you need to create a wonderful life for yourself. Your ability to steer your thoughts toward a destination of your own choosing is sufficient to enable you to overcome all obstacles, and make up for all limitations, on your road to success

The first thing successful people do is to change their mindset. I'm sorry if that sounds hippy-dippy to you. People who believe in themselves are more successful than people who don't, period! That observation begs the question, "How do I start to believe in myself?" For starters, you can let yourself off the hook. Nearly all of us have been trained since childhood to set very low expectations. Even the people who love us tell us to aim low. They don't want us to take chances. That's a shame, because taking chances teaches us that it's perfectly fine to take chances. Since we've been trained to set tiny, incremental goals if we set any goal at all, we have to retrain our brains to be more ambitious. We have to re-program our minds to feel that it's reasonable and normal to set huge, life-changing goals and then to achieve them. After all, if you set big goals, what's the worst thing that can happen?

If you succeed, it's magnificent. If you fail, you learn. There's really no such thing as failure. Other people can call you a failure if they want to, but who cares what other people think? One of the most common causes of failure is the habit of quitting when one is overtaken by temporary defeat. Every person is guilty of this mistake at one time or another. But I beg you never to quit in life. Allow yourself for flexibility. According to the Menninger Institute, the most significant quality that you will need to be successful in the twenty-first century is the quality of flexibility, especially in the way you think. Flexibility denotes your willingness to change and try new things. It especially means that you have the ability to continually abandon old, outmoded ideas in favor of new, more effective ideas. Many people spend much of their time arguing, rationalizing, and justifying their behaviours. They are determined to continue doing things the same old way even when it is perfectly clear that the old way no longer works. The way to avoid this tendency is to remain flexible, especially when you are most convinced that you are right.

If you step out into new territory every day, then it's familiar territory the next day and your reward for having learned something is that you get to be clueless about something new. Your house walls are thin. Office walls are thin, too. They can't protect us from reality. The only way to survive and thrive in this new-millennium workplace is to build yourself up from the inside. That means telling the truth and trying new things all the time.

The first step in reprogramming your mind for success is to get a journal. Start writing in your journal every day or whenever you get a moment. Everything that looks like a barrier to you is flimsy. You could knock every barrier down, but our obstacles look insurmountable from the ground level. You have to get altitude to see how easily every barrier in your way can be overcome.

There is no one to give you "A" grade. Your path is your biggest priority. Your current job is just a step on your path. You are wasting your precious mojo by caring too much about your relationship with your boss or your upcoming performance review. What difference does it make what your boss thinks about you?

Arise and Make a Difference; the Drive Behind Success

Your focus must be on your own path and your own goals. If your boss can help you take a step on your path, great! If not, there are plenty of other bosses who can. At some point you may decide the only boss you want to work for is yourself. That step will feel scary for a little while, too, and then it won't feel scary anymore. Write in your journal and envision the life you want; not an incremental step that seems desirable now only because it's a tiny improvement over your current situation.

Your mind can be your best friend or your worst enemy. Your thoughts alone have the power to make you healthy or sick, rich or poor, popular or unpopular. Your mind is like a powerful force that can be turned in any direction to bring about wonderful results, or wreak havoc and destruction. Your main goal in life must be to harness your amazing powers and direct them intelligently and systematically toward achieving everything you really want. Every system that was ever built can be torn down and improved upon. The system of fear and control that holds sway in so many workplaces are crumbling already. More and more working people are deciding they've had enough of kissing other people's rear ends to get crumbs. They are managing their own careers now. You can do the same thing!

You are stuck as long as you believe that other people are more powerful than you are. A nasty recruiter, an unhelpful HR person or a domineering manager have no power over you, but you have to feel that power in yourself. I can't convince you of it and neither can anybody else. One day, perhaps while you're writing in your journal, riding your bike or folding a load of laundry, you'll ask, "Why am I tolerating bad treatment?" There is no good answer, apart from "Who cares why I tolerated bad treatment this long; all I know is I'm not going to tolerate it anymore!"

Do you know you are more knowledgeable than you can imagine? Knowledge will not attract money, unless it is prearranged and intelligently directed, through practical plans of action, to the definite end of accumulation of money. Lack of understanding of this fact has been the source of confusion to millions of people who falsely believe that "knowledge is power." It is nothing of the sort! Knowledge is only potential power. It becomes power only when, and if, it is organized into definite plans of action, and directed to a definite end. This "missing link" in all systems of education known to civilization today may be found in the failure of educational institutions to teach their students how to organize and use knowledge after they acquire it. Many people make the mistake of assuming that because Henry Ford had but little "schooling," he is not a man of "education." Those who make this mistake do not know Henry Ford, nor do they understand the real meaning of the word "educate." That word is derived from the Latin word "*educo,*" meaning to educe, to draw out, to **develop from within.** An educated man is not, necessarily, one who has an abundance of general or specialized knowledge. An educated man is one who has so developed the faculties of his mind that he may acquire anything he wants, or its equivalent, without violating the rights of others.

You have to look in the mirror and ask, "Why am I making my boss more powerful than I am?" Maybe it's so that you can blame your boss for your frustration instead of owning up to the fact that it's hard to make changes and you've been avoiding the job search that will free you from the domineering manager. Tell yourself I need to become a boss of my own and strive towards its achievement. You are in charge of your life and career. You can take a step today to change whatever isn't working for you. Bad bosses will always be around us. We can blame them for our problems or step over, around or right through them the way you've dealt with other obstacles you've encountered and surmounted in your life so far. You are mighty now, and you are just getting started!

Anything you want good you can have it so claim it. Work hard to get it and when you get it reach back. Pull someone else's up, each one, teach one. You don't start to do something because of what you don't have. You don't start because you don't realize yet that the fruit of everything in life began with just a seed. Yes! You heard me right. Just a seed. Come on! Sow a variable seed now. That seed that can bear lasting fruit. What did I say? I said sow it now! Perhaps the most important quality of high-achieving men and women is that of ambition. They see themselves, think about themselves, and conduct themselves every day as though they were among the elite in their fields. They set high goals for themselves and continually work to exceed those goals. For them quotas are minimums, not maximums. They look upon the accomplishments of everyone else as challenges to themselves to be even better. And so, must you.

There is absolutely nothing easy in life. Everything that you must achieve must initially pass through a difficult tunnel. If you can go on to do the things that you hate doing then on the other side of it lies greatness. Never assume that you will get better in life one day. Assumptions are just psychological concepts. They are vague. Be realistic. Assumption is a huge disappointment in life. It's okay for people to call you names. Allow them to do so. They don't own you. You own your life. Don't ever be afraid of the reflection in the mirror. Gather enough courage and overcome them. Once you overcome them you are set for success. They won't last any longer. Just be patient and go through the pain of disgrace and embarrassment. Always remember that when you build an army you will have opposing forces. Keep yourself away from those who belittle your ambition in life. Small people with little mind does that but the great ones believe that you too can become great. Surround yourself with people who believe you but not those who don't believe in you. Get closer to people who even when they can't see it, they can see you.

What makes those who are successful now is because they were optimistic about the future. They never complain. They always try to solve the problems of others. You are a professional problem solver. Your success in your career is determined by how effectively you solve the problems and achieve the goals of your position. Never complain about your problems at work. You should be grateful for them. If you had no problems at work, you would have no job. When people become incapable to solve the problems that arise in their work, they are quickly replaced by people who can. When you become an exceptional problem solver, you are quickly promoted to solving even bigger and more important problems. From now on, see yourself as a problem solver. Your goal is to become absolutely excellent at solving any problem that the world can throw at you.

Opportunities always lies at where people complain. Yes! It's right there. So why don't you grab that opportunity amidst the several complains. Look, let no one deceive you or deceive yourself that there are no jobs in Ghana or your locality. Ask yourself is there anything I can do to make a difference? To make the difference you have to do the things that others don't do first. You have to make up first. You have to finish that homework, assignment, project, theses, quiz, first before any other person. Let everything you do meet the needs of others. To anybody tomorrow is now. Make the move, make the action now. Whether your family or friends believe this or not that is not important.

Make as many mistakes as you can. Take that risk now. When you fall rise up again. Yes! rise up again. That is your nature, that is how God created you. *"the righteous shall fall seven times but rise up again."* Don't worry about money. Human beings have idea problems not money problem. Why? Because it takes to generate wealth, money, and capital. Money follow people. You don't follow money. People follow their dreams. Nobody can conquer the world. We can only serve the world. Is either you work for others or you work for yourself. I choose to work for myself. How about you? Working for yourself simply implies that you are actually working for society. When others are smiling because of you then you are successful. People worry too much. They worry about the economy and politics. Be an opportunist and take advantage of their worry and make wealth. Dream for that now. Have a strong hope of its achievement. Because once you have hope, your family, your nation, and the entire world have hope. Always look at challenges as opportunities. Learn from other people's mistakes. Don't learn from their success stories.

It is only when you are experiencing the pressure of problems and obstacles that you are motivated to perform at your mental best. Facing and solving the inevitable problems and difficulties of life make you stronger and smarter, and bring out the very best in you. Most people do not understand the nature of problems. Problems are a normal and necessary part of life. They are inevitable and unavoidable. Problems come in spite of your best efforts to avoid them. Problems, therefore, come unbidden. The only part of a problem over which you have any control is your response to your problems. Effective people respond positively and constructively to problems. In this way, they demonstrate that they have developed high levels of "response-ability." They have developed the ability to respond effectively when unexpected or undesired difficulties occur.

Problems of all kinds bring out your very best qualities. They make you strong and resourceful. The more pressing your problems, and the more emotion you invest in solving those problems, the more creative you will become. Each time you solve a problem constructively, you become smarter and more effective. As a result, you prepare yourself for even bigger and more important problems to solve.

CHAPTER SIX

SUCCESS DEFINED

'Successful people do what unsuccessful people are not willing to do. Don't wish it were easier; wish you were better' (Jim Rohn)

The word success means differently to different people. To some people, success might be financial achievements, becoming a billionaire or millionaire for example. For some, it might be accolades. For sports men, it may mean getting plenty trophies, and medals. For some people also, being successful might simply achieving a state of wellness, health or happiness. I will also say that Success is you fulfilling the purpose for which you were created in life. Whatever it means to you, take notes of these ten habits of successful people. They apply to any area and any meaning of success.

#1. They set goals. You've probably never met a successful person who doesn't set goals. Because the chances of you finding what you want without a clear target to move forward are right around zero. If you don't know where you are going, you will end up at some place you didn't plan to be. Setting goals should be the first priority for anyone seeking success. Define exactly what it is you want-your end goals. Break down exactly what is required to get there. Set mini goals that can lead to the fulfillment of the large goal. Make sure your reasons of doing what you must do is very strong so that when you hit the roadblocks, when things go wrong as they always do, you have the strength and purpose to keep going.

#2. They take responsibility for their life. Another key habit of all successful people is their ability to take responsibility for the success and failures of their life. Unlike the majority, they never play the victim role. If something doesn't work out, they don't blame others. They learn the lesson. They learn one more way not to do something, and move on quickly. Your energy is best spent in the present, and planning for the future. Listen! Your thought processes should always be 'how can I make this work?' and 'what can I learn from this? Never live on the past or making excuses as to why you are not where you should be. Remember that everyone suffers some forms setbacks in their life so you are not left alone. Everyone has the opportunity to either blame others or circumstances, or to focus on moving on and creating a better future. Regardless of what had happened you decide what you do now.

#3. They have great self-discipline. As I discussed with you already as one of the keys to making a difference, discipline is a strong trait to all successful people, and it is one that can be developed with consistent use. Self-discipline is the most important feature in any life. Unless you put yourself under mental discipline, you will never develop the forces in you that are valuable to the commercial world. Rule your temper so that no matter what happens, what is said or done, your temper will be under absolute control. The man who does not rule his temper can never achieve the success that belongs to him. He destroys the building that he erects. Anyone that works from a home unsupervised by others knows the importance of self-discipline. When you are alone, will you choose to go through social media, watch cat videos on YouTube, or do something that will be very beneficial for your future? It is much easier to have self-discipline if you have clear goals and a meaningful purpose, something that is much more important than meaningless distractions.

#4. They are obsessed with self-development. You cannot really claim to be successful if you have given up working on yourself. Am not saying you are never satisfied in life. I mean you must know that it is human nature to want to grow and learn new things. Be open to learn new things and develop your mind through mentors, audio books and reading novels. Can I share with you the source of motivation that led to the production of this book you are reading now? This book in your hands now which as nice and eloquent as you can see it, was motivated by a mentor. Yes! I can still hear the motivational words of my uncle. "You can make it…you can be an author as long as you keep reading…the sky is your beginning…" He realized what is inside of me and encouraged me to read more because he knew I will become an author one day. What even drive me crazier was after reading his maiden book; *'Dare to Differ; the Niche in the Labyrinths of Life'.* I recommend that book to you to read. It will blow your mind and change your scope of perception of yourself. Hear me, the more you learn from mentors and books the more you will earn financially and even spiritually.

#5. They read a lot. Reading is a part and parcel of many successful people. The majority of people these days can't sit alone for a few minutes without becoming 'bored' picking up their phone to go on social media, probably to post about how bored they are such as "I am lonely…I am tired…I am bored…I need a companion…I am sick…I am in pains…I can't sleep…" and many more you might have also heard or seen on the social media. Successful people, however, are almost always happy to be alone. To be alone in quiet, to have the opportunity to read or listen to something that will benefit their mind and their future. If you are not a reader, try audio books. You can play them anywhere; in your room, lecture room, your office, or even in your car when travelling and use time that might normally be wasted to gain new skills and new strengths.

#6. They manage their time well. Time management is very essential to every successful person. Your inability to manage effectively every time available to you is your ability to fail. Unsuccessful people usually get stressed up and overwhelmed when there are too many tasks on their to-do list. Successful people are rarely abashed. They prioritize the long-pay off and most rewarding first, and leave the insignificant ones to last, knowing very well that it matters most to do the most valuable task first. Hear me! I started my national service with the same colleagues who graduated from the university. But not all of them thought of utilizing their time in the office to create something good out of themselves. But I did. I did make the difference by writing this book six months into the national service period. While others are watching movies from YouTube and enjoying themselves, I was busily reading online and typing this book. Successful people plan in advance, days, weeks, months ahead, knowing clearly what needs to be done to complete their jobs and reach their goals.

#7. They take risks. Successful people know that taking risk is part of their success. If you don't buy a university form, for instance, you cannot obtain any certificate. It's as simple as 'A B C D'. If you do not take big risks you cannot achieve big rewards. Successful people know that there will be time when they need to take risks in order to get to where they need to go. Often times, most people will not take those same risks for fear of failure. However, the greatest failure of successful people would be that of regret. The greatest failure in life is the fear of failing. My boss, risk going for the life you want, or guarantee living with the one you do not want.

#8. They keep going when they suffer failure and setbacks. We all suffer setbacks. Every single person who attempt to live their dream life will suffer through failure, many of them might even lose everything. Most quiet, the successful never quit. They keep going knowing their greatest character is fumed in adversity. Knowing their success story is being written in every moment, and it will be especially good now they have a comeback story.

#9. They find a way to win. In the midst of many loosing opportunity is also better opportunity to win. This is what successful people are known for. Successful people find a way. Period! Whatever life throws their way, they deal with it, dodge it, smash through, whatever is required they find a way to win. It's about the whatever it takes mentality. It is the confidence in knowing whatever happens, I will give my all and leave nothing on the table. I will find a way to win! Hear me, what does not kill you will actually make you strong. If living a successful life was easy, I am sure many people will be successful.

#10. They do what they love. If you are not doing what you love, you cannot actually claim yourself a success. Spending the majority of your working hours, that's the majority of your life, doing things you hate, for money, is not successful living. It is torture to the soul and the mind. If you need to suffer for doing something you do not like to get to a life you love, do that but do not lose sight of exactly that; your main purpose. Find your life purpose. Think of all the things you love to do more than anything in the world, then brainstorm how you can turn those passions into profit and doing what you love every day. do what you love every day and you will never work a day in your life. Self-made millionaires almost invariably say that their secret of success was that they found out what they enjoyed doing, and they did it with their whole heart.

Most successful people feel that they don't really work at all. Some of them say, "I haven't worked a day in my life." Their work and their play are intermingled. They don't know where one begins and the other ends. When they are not at work, they think about it and talk about it. And when they are at work, they lose themselves in it.

What changes people is when all your; **'should'** become a **'must'**. Don't say I should work, I should go, I should do it… say I must work, I must go, I must do it. Unless you take some new actions, unless you start thinking some new thoughts, unless you start having some conversations, unless you have the got to create out some new things, you cannot be successful.

He that cannot stand being talked about is not ready for the limelight. It is stars, that people talk about. Every single person who has not done anything worthwhile or exceptional or difficult or extraordinary- whether mathematicians, scientists, everyone of such people encounter some difficult times. There is no easy road. No, it's not possible. Everyone has an issue. Everyone has a hard road. If you don't fall you don't get better. Everyone has a unique seed in him/her that matures to become a strong tree. Can I ask you this; what kind of tree is inside you? That seed is who you are. You were not born to get job and pay bills and die. You were not born to work and retire and then get some penny for pension allowance. You and I were born to make this world a better place. If you want a better life tomorrow, you need to start working on it now.

Desire is thought impulse. Thought impulses are forms of energy. When you begin with the thought impulse of a desire to accumulate money, you are drafting into your service the same "stuff" that Nature used in creating this earth, and every material form in the universe, including the body and brain in which the thought impulses function. The starting point of all achievement is desire. Keep this constantly in mind. Weak desires bring weak results, just as a small amount of fire makes a small amount of heat. If you find yourself lacking in persistence, this weakness may be remedied by building a stronger fire under your desires.

I wish could repeat it over and over again, so that, wherever you turned in this book, your eyes would see this one fact: You have within you all of the qualities and elements that are necessary to make you a success. Your chief work is the development of the thing that nature has already given you. Before you go to the office, or any work place, create all around you and in you an atmosphere of victory. You go out with the consciousness that you have victory. You and the unseen one is going down to the office together and you are going to put it over. You are going out after that job with the smile of a victor not the smile of a man who is trying to smile, but the man who smiles in spite of himself. If it is mental work, think every problem through. Be the one man in that office or workplace where you work who thinks through on every problem that comes up. You will find that the boss will want you. Very few men have the ability to think through. They guess, they speculate, they theorize. But down yonder behind the desk is the man who takes the problem and resolutely drives himself to think through that problem from every angle. The boss can get men to do what he tells them to do. He is looking for one with ability to tell the others how to do it. So, set the standard high for yourself. Have a lofty spiritual ideal. Climb up to it.

Between you and it there may be many a swamp through which a road must be made. Loggers always build roads for the timber they wish to market. You will have to build a road to market your abilities. There is pain and fatigue ahead of you, but you must dress for the job. Remember to associate yourself with people who have won, those who help you climb to the top. Don't hang around with a group of "has been." Associate with the men who are climbing up. The idle, gossiping people will not help you. The lazy and careless will stand in your way. Those who spend their nights in the road house or at the gambling hall will never help you. Don't think you can get something for nothing. Put your money where it will count. Put your time where it will pay you dividends. This battle is not for the thoughtless, heedless guesser or uncompromising dreamer. It is for the man who works

We are here laying the foundation for the demonstration of a fact of great importance to the person who does not comprehend why some people appear to be "lucky" while others of equal or greater ability, training, experience, and brain capacity, seem destined to ride with misfortune. This fact may be elucidated by the statement that every human being has the ability to completely control his own mind, and with this control, obviously, every person may open his mind to the tramp thought impulses which are being released by other brains, or close the doors tightly and admit only thought impulses of his own choice. Nature has endowed man with absolute control over but one thing, and that is thought. This fact, coupled with the additional fact that everything which man creates begins in the form of a thought, leads one very near to the principle by which fear may be mastered. If it is true that all thought has a tendency to clothe itself in its physical equivalent (and this is true, beyond any reasonable room for doubt), it is equally true that thought impulses of fear and poverty cannot be translated into terms of courage and financial gain.

The people of America began to think of poverty, following the Wall Street crash of 1929. Slowly, but surely that mass thought was crystalized into its physical equivalent, which was known as a "depression." This had to happen; it is in conformity with the laws of Nature. Put the company for which you work under obligation to you. Keep society under obligation to you. The world's greatest scientists, chemists, and mechanics, engineers have all put the world in debt to them. Be a real contributor to your age. Don't just exist. Mothers, give to the world some great sons and daughters. Put your best into their training. You have no idea how dependent the world is upon mothers. Make the world a better place, because you lived in it and played your part. Selfishness cramps ability. Be bigger than the blunders that you make. Live big. Be big in your dreams, in all things that you do. Learn to love men. Only lovers count. Give to the world better service with every added year. Forgive your enemies. Never go to their level and hate with them. The lying and opposition of your enemies is your diploma. Give a heaping measure in all your ministry. God is the original giver. Be in His class

CHAPTER SEVEN

BECOMING SUCCESSFUL

"No one can cheat you out of ultimate success but yourself." - Ralph Waldo Emerson

Let me start by re-echoing what Myles Munroe said. *"If you want to become successful in life do not seek success but rather be a person of value"*. In other words, make yourself valuable and they will pay for. That is exactly what we do with gold, silver, and water. Our society have made these things valuable so we pay a lot of money for them because we have made them valuable. So, make yourself just like a gold. In other words, develop a gift in your life that has become valuable to everybody else that they will pay you to perform. What will people think about you when they mention your name? What do you think of Archbishop Duncan William? Prayer, right? Joel Osteen- motivational speaker right. What about Benson Idahosa, Benin Hinn, Billy Graham, Kathryn Colman, Jack Ma, Mark Zukerberg…?

Become so good in an area that they can't ignore you. The world is full of general people but you must cease to become general. You've got to rise up and decide now that in the next two, five, ten, twenty years I am going to curve out a niche for myself. Hear me! Jesus sounded valuable when he said " I am the bread and water of life" of which no one can live eternally without eating and drinking it respectively.

Arise and Make a Difference; the Drive Behind Success

So, you read all about the success of other individuals. You got lost in the world of tips, tricks, and courses for success. None of them worked for you. At the end of it you were still left wondering, "what is it that I don't have?" You're still looking now. You've exhausted your edition of Outliers by Malcolm Gladwell. You've been through hours of listening to those motivational coaches say, "never give up, and you'll get what you want!" You've done it all, and nothing is working. You're sick of it, right? You want something that you can start doing right now. You don't want the "never give up" speech again. So here is the reality.

Success is something within you. It's your daily habit. Your morning routines. What you spend your time doing. It's not these tips and tricks that others try to tell you, it's the way you view the world! It is not every closed door that is locked. Go check it up before you conclude. Hear me! Even closed doors still have keys. True or false? Why not look for the keys to those closed doors rather than drawing baseless conclusions in life. Don't give up hope. Permit me to give you some nuggets to push you onto the path of success.

To begin with, start to accept changes. Change is the one constant you can rely on in life. When all else fails you, you can bet that change will be lurking around the corner. With this in mind, wouldn't it be a smart thing to finally squash that fear of change all together? Listen! Change is not easily achieved. But make your mind to change. Change your thinking. Change your attitude!

Change your unsupportive friends! Change your environment! If possible, change your name!

Successful people are able to adapt to change. They need to be. If one idea fails, which many will, the successful mind can take that and adapt to the changes presented by the situation. But how do you accept change? The way you always have, you just get on with it. Know that it's there, it's happening all the time, and don't let it catch you off-guard. Plan for it, expect it, embrace it, and use it to your advantage. Many highly successful people are often described as "loners." However, this does not mean "a-loners." They are not isolated, and antisocial individuals. They are loners in that they are highly selective about who they spend time with. They do not drink coffee with whoever is sitting there, or go out for lunch with whoever happens to be walking out the door at the same time. They carefully build and maintain high-quality relationships, and they fastidiously avoid negative people who might hold them back.

Successful and happy people have a generally positive mental attitude. Prosperous and wealthy people have a prosperous and wealthy mind-set. Kind, patient, gentle, loving people, who enjoy happy and fulfilling relationships with their families and friends, have kind, patient, loving ways of thinking. When you develop the same mind-set that other successful people have, you will soon enjoy the same results and experiences that they do. You have complete control over only one thing in the universe; **your thinking!** You can decide what you are going to think in any given situation. Your thoughts and the way you interpret any event trigger your feelings; positive or negative. If associating with positive people is a key to success, then the flip side is for you to get away and keep away from negative or "toxic" people. Negative people are the primary source of most unhappiness. Problems with such people are most likely your major sources of stress and frustration. Negative people do more to diminish your joy in life than any other single factor.

Your thoughts and feelings lead to your actions and determine the results you get. It all starts with your thoughts. Successful people are those who *think* more effectively than unsuccessful people. They approach their lives, relationships, goals, problems, and experiences differently from others. They sow better seeds, and as a result they reap better lives. If you learn to think and act like other successful, happy, healthy, and prosperous people, you will soon enjoy the kind of lives they do. When you change your thinking, you change your life.

William James, a famous psychologist, said, 'the greatest revolution of the 21st century is the discovery that by changing the inner attitudes of your mind, you can change the other aspects of your life.'
Start to set goals; Not just any goals, but SMART goals. That is goals that are Specific, Measurable, Achievable, Relevant, and Time bound. You know when you draw up a check-list, and you tick each individual little job off it? Think back to the feeling of each of those ticks. Think about how relieving it is. Think about how empowered

and motivated you feel for the next job. It's a pretty damn good feeling, right? Then staring at that completed list at the end of the day, knowing that you've accomplished everything you wanted to do for that day. Make your goals that size. Reach your goals every day. Allow that momentum to build, and empower you, every single day! (But don't forget to schedule your empty check-list days too.)

A goal that you have not yet achieved is merely a problem that you have not yet solved. This is why success has been defined as *the ability to solve problems*. If you are not earning the kind of money that you would like, that is an unsolved problem. If you are not enjoying the levels of health and fitness that you desire, this is just a problem that you must solve. An obstacle that stands between you and your goal is merely a problem waiting for a solution. Any limitation that is holding you back is just another problem waiting for you to solve. In every case, your job is to not let the problem get on top of you, but rather for you to get on top of the problem.

Start to commit to things; Get rid of those commitment fears. If you want to be successful, you have to commit to things. A new job, a new partner, a new exercise regime, a new magazine subscription, whatever it is; you need to commit! Stop the procrastination if you really want to become successful! "Old Man Procrastination" stands within the shadow of every human being, waiting for his opportunity to spoil one's chances of success. Most of us go through life as failures, because we are waiting for the "time to be right" to start doing something worthwhile. Do not wait. The time will never be "just right." Start where you stand, and work with whatever tools you may have at your command, and better tools will be found as you go along.   If you can't commit when things are going well, you're going to abandon that vehicle and run a mile the moment you hit some turbulence. This won't lead you to success. It can't. You're not sticking around long enough to reach it. There's no real easy way to do this. Though weighing up the cost of the commitment versus the rewards can often be a good start. Regardless, however you decide to face up to it, the end result is the same. You start committing.

Start to identify your purpose; A purpose is the fast-track to success. With your purpose in mind, much like the achievable goals, all that hard work seems a lot more appealing to overcome. God made it so explicit when He spoke to the prophet Jeremiah; *"I know the plans I have for you; plans of good not evil, to give you a successful end..."* God has a purpose for you. There is a purpose for which you have been created. If you have no idea of what your purpose is then start now to discover your purpose. Go to the manual of your creation- God, to find out. When things get rough you can just sit there and say, "Why are you doing this again?" and your purpose will always serve as the motivation you need. Ask yourself these questions; Who am I? What do I want from life? What is it I have that others will benefit from receiving?

How am I going to get there? These are just but a few questions to lead you to the path of fulfilling your purpose.

Start to cultivate patience; Another timeless piece of advice, inexcusable to leave out of anything discussing success. You need to have patience. Yes, some things can happen overnight, but these are often the smaller successes. It doesn't matter what it is you want to achieve, knowing how to wait will be a part of it. A successful blog doesn't launch with thousands of subscribers overnight. A powerful novel doesn't get written in a day. A superstar fitness model doesn't miraculously gain his or her physique in 24 hours. Success takes time. You just have to keep taking every step you can towards it. How I wished I could have completed this book and publish it within a month or so. But I cultivated the spirit pf patience and this is how far it brought me. This novel you are reading now is birthed out of patience.

Start to identify your downfalls; No successful mind is successful if it cannot see where it falls short. It is only in the identification of the shortcoming that it could ever have the potential to be addressed. Many people are their own worst critic though, so it's not hard to see what needs work. The hard part is putting in the work. Knowing you're lazy and doing something about the laziness are two different things. To be successful you would have to identify that laziness, and then adopt a proactive solution to it. Just saying, "yeah I'm lazy," isn't going to get the work done. The last, and maybe the hardest, part to it all is showing yourself compassion. You're not going to get it absolutely perfect first try. That's okay. You've got a lot of time left. As long as you're actually doing something about your downfalls, other than complaining, you're probably ahead of most people.

Start to identify the growth in 'failure'; Do you know what almost every successful person has in common? They've failed. Jack Ma was denied admission to Harvard University ten times. Yes 10 times! Dr. Seuss was rejected by 27 publishers. Stephen King threw his career-launching manuscript in the trash, though luckily his wife pulled it out. Walt Disney was told he had no imagination. Did any of these people give up? NO! They didn't give up! Type in the names of the aforementioned or any other successful person you know and see what is behind their success. The only thing stopping you from trying again is you.

Start to practice emotional creativity; Emotional creativity, better known as empathy, is the backbone of success. To be able to relate, to put yourself in someone else's shoes, is what makes you a successful human being. There're various reasons why, such as: To be able to serve people what it is they want, which is the key to many successful businesses and careers, you have to relate to their situation. If you lack the emotional creativity to empathize with their situation, you won't connect well with them. If you're on your pursuit for success and you're going to have to climb over some people's heads, how are you going to stay with human doing that? By relating to them. Are you willing to crush other people to get where you want to be? Can you live with that decision?

You'll only know by empathizing. Successful people, at least many of them, are likable. They're likable because you can relate to them. You can relate because they're creative enough, emotionally, to appeal to you! In addition, empathy makes you a better human being overall. Putting yourself in someone's situation is going to lead to better behavior, from you, when it comes to dealing with said people. If you're not sold on empathy, just read some novels of Psychology.

David Cuschieri said, *"the mind is a powerful force. it can enslave us or empower us. it can plunge us into the depths of misery or take us to the heights of ecstasy. learn to use the power wisely."*

Start to meditate; With the madness of success comes the desperate need for peace. As a successful person, you'll likely be making stressful decisions every day. If you can't manage that stress, it will dominate you. So, take a couple of minutes out of your day, and really let go. Hit the pause button on everything. It will all still be there when you come back, but find time to really just be with yourself. Otherwise that stress could eat you alive.

So, there it is. Now all you've got to do is put them into practice. Are you ready for success? How is your memory? Is your cognitive function as strong as you'd like it to be? If not, then you're definitely going to be interested in the memory improvement tips I will be sharing with you. Despite what you might think or have been told; improving your ability to recall information is certainly possible. You just need to know the right ways to do it. So how to improve memory? Let's dive straight into the first of seven easy ways to improve your memory significantly.

1. Meditate; We live in a world of non-stop, 24/7 information. It's like a waterfall that is endlessly pouring news, data, facts and figures into our conscious minds. Unfortunately, our brains are not designed to absorb this tremendous amount of information. It's no wonder then, that most people struggle to remember information and recall things. Even if you believe you have a good memory and are comfortable with multi-tasking, you will also be aware that there is only so much information your brain can process at one time. And research suggests that the more information and distractions, the harder it is for you to transfer information to your long-term memory. Fortunately, meditation can help you out. Even if you just meditate for 10 minutes per day, you will boost your ability to focus, which in turn, will make it easier for you to remember important facts. And don't forget, meditation doesn't just have to be closing your eyes and sitting in an upright position. Some people prefer to simply take a short walk in nature. This clears and calms their mind, and still provides the all-important boost to their focus.

2. Get plenty of sleep; If you are sleep deprived or have not been sleeping well, then I'm guessing you're not remembering well either. This is because sleep and memory are intimately connected. If you have a busy life and regularly find yourself not getting enough sleep, then this will negatively impact your cognitive abilities —

including your memory. How much sleep should you be getting? Well, according to the National Sleep Foundation, you need a minimum of seven to nine hours of sleep per night. If you get this amount of sleep regularly, then within just a few days, you will see a tangible improvement to your ability to remember and recall things. Now, I will be honest with you, maintaining a proper sleep cycle is not always easy (especially when the latest Netflix series has just been released!). But if you care about improving your short-term and long-term ability to remember things, then it's critical that you try to get at least the recommended amount of sleep every night. Sleeping is a precious activity. It regenerates your body, clears your mind, and helps with the storing and retrieval of information. However, don't sleep just yet, as I want to tell you about another great way to increase memory…

3. Challenge your brain; When was the last time you challenged your brain? I don't mean challenged in the sense of overeating or under sleeping. I'm referring to stretching your mental capabilities through things like crossword puzzles, Sudoku and memory games. To expand your memory bank, and to make your recall razor-sharp, you need to continually challenge your brain. If you normally spend a chunk of your week playing computer games, then instead of shooting and killing your enemies, why not let some of them live while you put your attention into boosting your brain power! Challenging your brain will strengthen your neural pathways and enhance your mental abilities. But don't just take my word for it, try one of the apps above and see the positive benefits for yourself.

4. Take more breaks; Taking regular breaks is the best way to keep yourself productive, creative and alive to opportunities. It's also the best way to learn new information. Let me explain. Typically, when studying lots of new information, most people will spend hours reading it in an attempt to learn and remember the content as quickly as possible. Unfortunately, they've overlooked something. It's similar to physical exercise. You wouldn't attempt to train vigorously for five or so hours in a row. Instead, you'd take regular breaks to give your lungs, heart and muscles adequate time to recover. Failing to do this will result in muscle cramps and overexertion. It's the same with your brain. If you overload it with information, you will suffer from mental fatigue. Make sure you take regular breaks when learning new information. I recommend at least a 10-minute break every hour. If you don't want to be as regimented as that, then take breaks as soon as you find yourself losing the ability to focus on the new material. That is exactly how I do my studies. Your brain will thank you and your learning aptitude will move up a level.

5. Learn a new skill; I love this quote, *"Learning never exhausts the mind."* – Leonardo da Vinci. Imagine you work for a global financial institution in one of their call centers. You take over 100 calls a day many of them complaints. When you started the job a few months back, you were excited to be in full-time employment and working for a household name. Unfortunately, your initial enthusiasm quickly turned into frustration.

The endless complaint calls began to take their toll on you. And the supervisors irritated you too, as they were far too interested in micro-managing you rather than letting you work in your own way. Now, in the story above, the ending could be that you put up with a job you didn't like, and led a dull and frustrated working life for years and years. However, an alternative ending is this: you channeled your dissatisfaction in to learning a new skill (computer coding). It took you a year or two to get up to speed, but it allowed you to successfully upgrade your career and the ongoing learning made the call center job much more bearable. Clearly, learning new skills gives you impetus, focus and something to aim for. Your brain loves to learn, and you should tap into this by always seeking our new information. And when learning becomes a habit, you'll find your ability to remember and recall things effortlessly, becomes a habit too.

6. Start working out; If you are not already working out regularly, then here is another reason to do so. Exercising for 20-30 minutes three times a week will improve your long-term memory. Regular exercise increases blood flow in your body and supplies the brain with extra oxygen and nutrients. And a well-nourished brain is a well-functioning brain! "But I just don't have the time?" I hear you say. Not a problem. A research has shown that a daily burst of 60 seconds of high-intensity exercise, offered many of the benefits of the longer exercise routines. So, if you're short on time now you know what to do. Interested in getting started?

7. Eat healthier foods; I'm sure you've heard the expression: "You are what you eat." This applies to your brain too. The food that you eat helps determine your brain's capacity to store and recall information. A poor diet (think junk food + soda!) harms not just your physical health, but your mental health too. Fortunately, there are several foods that are especially good for your brain and your memory. These include: blueberries, celery and dark chocolate. But anything high in antioxidants will have a positive effect on your brain and memory. Conversely, highly-processed foods and those loaded with sugar will have a negative impact on your memory. This is due to them providing insufficient nutrients for your brain leading you to easily suffer from mental fatigue.

Final thoughts; I sincerely hope these seven memory boosting ways that I've covered in this write up will be of help to you. You don't need to implement them all. I suggest just trying the ones that appeal to you. But, if you're serious about dramatically improving your memory, then make a start right now on adopting one or more of the ways I've suggested. I'm confident you won't regret it.

Nurture Your Mind

"You might be poor, your shoes might be broken, but your mind is a palace."
Frank McCourt, Angela's Ashes.

Most problems result from your thoughts about a situation outside of your control. Allow me to unpack this in more detail. Reflect on an area of life causing you frustration. What if you were to hand it to an outsider and ask them to assess it from their perspective? Would they feel the same about it? Of course not, because they are less invested in it than you are. Therein lies the problem. Your attachment to unpleasant circumstances blinds you to seeing it from another viewpoint. What if there is a better way of taking ownership of your thoughts? *"The mind is everything. What you think, you become,"* Buddha wrote. Your self is nothing more than what you believe it to be. *"You must remove all the internal and external definitions of self that limit your progress in life,"* writes author Jay Samit in: *'Disrupt Yourself'*. Since you cannot see your thoughts until they manifest into reality, you may question whether you contributed to your problem. The mind is a powerful ally or foe. I liken it to the tale of the *Two Wolves Within and The One You Feed.* You can feed the good wolf or the bad wolf. Either way, your mind should be tamed with the right stimuli if you want to experience greater success. It was the late American motivational speaker Zig Ziglar who said: *"People often say that motivation doesn't last. Well, neither does bathing, that's why we recommend it daily."*

Therefore, nurture your mind with empowering thoughts if you want it to become a powerful asset. Author Jay Samit believes we often hold ourselves back from the success we deserve: "The unfortunate reality is that what holds most people back is actually their own belief that they are not good enough or deserving enough to be successful."

Unconscious Thoughts

"The mind is not a vessel to be filled, but a fire to be kindled."—Plutarch.

It's no secret that everything out there in your world begins at the level of the mind, as thoughts. The Hermetic aphorism states: "As within, so without." What you hold in mind will become your reality whether you like it or not. This is empowering because it allows you to become the architect of your life, not a mere spectator of your destiny. If you are unconscious to your thoughts or carrying unresolved childhood traumas, they are likely to manifest somewhere in your future.

Carl Jung, a psychiatrist, said *"Your vision will become clear only when you can look into your own heart. Who looks outside, dreams; who looks inside, awakes."* The greatest minds in history knew that success results from mental discipline and knowing one's self at a deeper level. Nisargadatta Maharaj, an Indian spiritual teacher of non-duality, said: *"There is nothing to practice. To know yourself, be yourself. To be yourself, stop imagining yourself to be this or that. Just be. Let your true nature emerge. Don't disturb your mind with seeking."* Many people don't know what they want until it shows up in their life, at which point it's not as they imagined. Similarly, their reality is built around unconscious thoughts because they are unaware, they exist. They are not clear on their ambitions or dreams but are pulled along by life, hoping they will end up where they need to be. This is the person who proclaims: "There's a reason for everything," but has no clue what the reason is. "By taking just five minutes each morning to visualize success, you train your brain to accept that you are capable of handling success. By visualizing each step of your journey, you are actually getting your mind prepared to handle the opportunity," avows Jay Samit once more. For example, most people want to be in a healthy relationship and have a list of qualities their ideal partner should have. They might attract their romantic interest after a while since they have devoted enough of their attention and energy to it. However, once the partner enters their life if the individual has not reconciled their unconscious thoughts from the past it is likely to cause problems in the relationship since the other person will mirror their insecurities.

Develop a Greater Sense of Self

"There is nothing more important to true growth than realizing that you are not the voice of the mind—you are the one who hears it."
Michael A. Singer.

The self-aware person draws to himself circumstances consistent with their highest self, instead of satisfying their egos' needs. To discipline your mind, develop a greater sense of self by focusing on your self-development. You've heard it said, success is the by-product of the person you become. The self-aware person spends years developing their strengths while mindful of their weaknesses. The late American minister and author Norman Vincent Peale wrote: *"Formulate and stamp indelibly on your mind a mental picture of yourself as succeeding. Hold this picture tenaciously. Never permit it to fade. Your mind will seek to develop the picture… do not build up obstacles in your imagination."* In her acclaimed book *Mindsight,* Stanford psychologist Carol Dweck identifies a person as having either a fixed mindset or a growth mindset. A person with a fixed mindset believes intelligence is static. They are absorbed in their problems instead of seeing them as an opportunity to be overcome. In contrast, the person with a growth mindset considers intelligence can be developed through nurturing and discipline. "This growth mindset is based on the belief that your basic qualities are things you can cultivate through your efforts.

Although people may differ in every which way; in their initial talents and aptitudes, interests, or temperaments; everyone can change and grow through application and experience," affirms Carol Dweck in *Mindset: How You Can Fulfil Your Potential.* Positive thinking does not improve your situation because it is merely a smoke screen for what is simmering below the surface. The key to greater success is to integrate the fractured aspects of your character into the wholeness of your being. To discipline the mind, focus on what you wish to see in your world. Hold an unrelenting commitment to make that your reality. You will be pushed to your limits at times and your inner resolve will be tested. However, your investment in your personal growth will be of great service during these times. Success in life results from forging the mind just as a blacksmith tempers hot steel, fabricating it into a finished product. Albert Einstein, an eminent theoretical physicist said, *"we can't solve problems by using the same kind of thinking we used when we created them."* After all, if you wish to attain greater success, you must develop a new mind. A new paradigm in which to perceive the world around you, instead of being at the mercy of your unconscious mind.

Hear me, its high time you choose the right direction. Sometimes humans are over thinking about their lives. Everybody wants to be successful, yet they go experimenting, trying to pick many paths at a time, expecting that at least they may reach one goal. But the fact is that only few people succeed in their life with many dreams. A successful person is someone who visualizes and chooses the path he or she is capable of! This is how you will meet your expectation and imagination. Visualize yourself about the things you want to achieve with ease, efficiency, and supreme confidence. The path that you choose must be something realistic and remind yourself of the fact that you should learn to grow and fly high. But all thing you must do with consistency and discipline.

There is a great orator who does not attain to greatness, until he closes his eyes and begins to rely entirely upon the faculty of Creative Imagination. When asked why he closed his eyes just before the climaxes of his oratory, he replied, "I do it, because then I speak through ideas which come to me from within." One of America's most successful and best-known financiers followed the habit of closing his eyes for two or three minutes before making a decision. When asked why he did this, he replied, "With my eyes closed, I am able to draw upon a source of superior intelligence." The major difference between the genius and the ordinary "crank" inventor, may be found in the fact that the genius works through his faculty of creative imagination, while the "crank" knows nothing of this faculty. The scientific inventor (such as Mr. Edison, and Dr. Gates), makes use of both the synthetic and the creative faculties of imagination. For example, the scientific inventor or "genius" begins an invention by organizing and combining the known ideas or principles accumulated through experience, through the synthetic faculty (the reasoning faculty). If he finds this accumulated knowledge to be insufficient for the completion of his invention, he then draws upon the sources of knowledge available to him through his creative faculty.

Grab Your Opportunities to Achieve; Time and tide, they say wait for one. Spend a few minutes doing meditation and exercising your mind. It makes you feel relaxed and develop your mind power. Always have a strong positive feeling to your goal that one day you will succeed, not immediately but slowly and definitely. Opportunities can knock at your door any time and at any moment, but to grab that; you should be well programmed about your desire to your subconsciousness. When you have got a smart and smooth subconscious mind, you are on the way to your success. Because all you will gain is you will be able to grow up as a constructive and productive individual to do a potential work in accordance to your path or goal.

Your most valuable asset is your time, and relationships with people are enormously time-consuming. The number of high-quality relationships you can form and maintain is limited. There are simply not enough hours in the day or enough days in the month. You must be selective about the people with whom you associate. You must choose them carefully. Baron de Rothschild, in his *"Maxims for Success"*, said, *"Make no useless acquaintances."* This may sound a bit cold, but remember, your life is precious, and your life is made up of the minutes and hours of each day. You cannot afford to squander it on relationships with people whom you cannot help, and who cannot help you either, to live and enjoy a better life. You must guard your time judiciously. As Benjamin Franklin wrote, *"Dost thou love life? Then do not squander time; for that's the stuff life is made of."*

Everything that matters in life is to have a right subconscious mind, the faith to carry it out, and the willingness to be grateful to achieve your goal. Whenever you deal with dreams, you should be a smart worker and most importantly, you must learn from your mistakes and grow out of it to taste your success! You are capable of more than you know, start to develop yourself, start to re-program your mind and don't just settle for the so-called normal life. The majority of people are not going to work because they want to, it is because they have to pay their bills. Is that what the purpose of work is? To pay your bills? If money was not an issue what would you do with your life? How would you truly like to live your life? What is your answer? Everyone has an answer for these questions, but the question is what are you spending your days doing? Are you living a life like the majority of people?

Everything which man creates begins in the form of a thought impulse. Man can create nothing which he does not first conceive in thought. Through the aid of the imagination, thought impulses may be assembled into plans. The imagination, when under control, may be used for the creation of plans or purposes that lead to success in one's chosen occupation. All thought impulses, intended for transmutation into their physical equivalent, voluntarily planted in the subconscious mind, must pass through the imagination, and be mixed with faith. The "mixing" of faith with a plan or purpose, intended for submission to the subconscious mind, may be done only through the imagination.

It doesn't matter about your past, it doesn't matter how young or old you are, it doesn't matter how you done in school, it doesn't matter what you did not do, and it doesn't matter how many failures you have encountered. You can achieve anything. Turn the page and rewrite a new script, don't let the first chapter of your life determine the rest of your life.

The Conscious Mind; Your conscious mind is where you do your thinking and your planning it's the place of logic. Picture this. Your conscious mind is like the driver at the wheel of a crane; it directs and controls the crane, but it does not perform any of the actual work. Your conscious mind is the driver at the wheel of your incredibly powerful subconscious mind. So, what does that mean for you? Have you ever tried to change a habit; such as quitting smoking or losing weight; using sheer willpower? If you have, then you know willpower is a poor strategy for creating lasting change in your life. Because willpower originates in the conscious mind and is therefore limited in its capabilities. When you attempt to use your willpower to make a change, you are only using 1 to 5 percent of your resources to accomplish an already undesirable outcome!

Learning to effectively utilize your conscious mind to direct your subconscious mind is what living your best life is. Top performers have learned how to do this, but whether they can articulate how they do it is another question altogether. This is the challenge before you that, once mastered, will allow you to design your life. My boss, have control of your mind now! Many are the things you are and will be missing in your life if you don't pay critical attention to your mind. I hope you still remember the sub topic you are reading now? It is '**the mind as the originator of success'**. Do you want to be successful in life? Then turn and pay attention to the message your mind is telling you.

I know that success belongs to every one of us. We may not be great financiers or great authors, but in our place in life we may know that we have won. It is necessary that we make the right choice, find out what our talents and abilities are and have them properly trained and fitted to achieve the desired end. There are a few things that are absolutely imperative if we are to fulfill our part of life's program. There must be a purpose from which we cannot be swerved. There must be the right kind of companionship. The wrong kind of associates are a serious handicap, but it can be overcome. Some of us will be handicapped with physical environments that seem almost unsurmountable, but we can conquer. Wow! All too soon we have come to the end of this chapter. Congratulations! I hope you are enjoying the reading. Having read about how useful the mind is to making a difference and becoming successful, let me usher you to another amazing chapter of this book. Enjoy yourself with its flavours.

CHAPTER EIGHT

THE EARLY MORNING PROCLAMATION

"If you paint in your mind a picture of bright and happy expectations, you put yourself into a condition conducive to your goals"
Norman Vincent Peale

Every morning when you wake up and your feet hit the floor, tell yourself today is today. Today is the day that I will be at my peak. Today is the day I will set my life up to win. Today is the day I will set my future up for success. Today I will give my all every minute, every moment with everyone I encountered. To live the great life, you've got to get your mornings right.

Don't just wonder out of bed and throw yourself aimlessly into the drama of this world. Get up with purpose and develop a routine that works for you. Work out! Get your body moving. Be grateful to God. Spend at least some few minutes in appreciation for all the things you do have and for the opportunities that are coming your way today. Say thank you! Say thank you for this day. Thank you for keeping me alive and healthy. Thank God for your family, your dreams, your past, the opportunities coming your way today. Declare with me, 'I am ready for action'. Good!

The Law of Expectations says that *whatever you expect, with confidence, becomes your own self-fulfilling prophecy*. You are constantly telling your own fortune when you talk about how you think things are going to turn out in a particular area. Your expectations then determine your attitude, and your attitude causes people to behave toward you in a way that reflects what you are thinking inside. If your expectation is to become successful, you will eventually be successful. If your expectation is to become happy and popular, you will be happy and popular. If you expect to be healthy and prosperous, admired and respected by the people around you, that is what will happen.

You can tell your true expectations by listening to the words you use to describe an upcoming event. Always think and talk positively about the future. Start every morning by saying; *"I believe something wonderful is going to happen to me today."* Then, throughout the day, expect the best. Be open and alert to the possibility that each thing that happens, positive or negative, contains something good. You will be astonished at the effect this approach to life has on your attitude, and on the way, you are treated by the people around you.

When you wake up in the morning, set your goals and intentions for the day. You cannot reach the most sought of destination without knowing what that place is. Ask yourself, what I am going to accomplish today? What miracles are you going to create today? Write them down. Believe you can and get to work. Start your day with power and intentions and live your life with strength and direction. This is your day take control of how you react to everything today. Declare that today I will plant seeds for my future. Today I am alive, grateful and I will look for the good. Today I will notice opportunities and execute them. Visualize what you want from today and work towards it. Believe that great things are coming. Meditate and clear your mind of all negativity. This is your day. set your life off to win. How you start your day often determines how you live your day. how you start your day often determines your future. How you start your day consistently determine the quality of your life. You must set up a morning routine that gets you strong. Ask yourself the most important question; 'if today was my last day on this earth how would I want to live? What examples will I set? Never let your dreams go up in smoke.

In order to stay on top of your job or career, you should read in your field at least one hour per day, underlining and taking good notes. Anything less than one hour per day will put you in danger of being passed by your competitors. Work at least as hard on yourself as you do on your job. Do this every day. let it be your habit. At the very least, you should get up every morning and read 30 to 60 minutes in something educational and inspirational like this novel you are reading now. Isn't it inspiring you? Take careful notes. Review your notes on a regular basis. Reflect on what you have learned, and think about how you could apply the new ideas in your daily life.

Use your powers of visualization to imagine yourself using the new information in some way. This will dramatically increase the speed at which you learn and retain the new ideas, and increase the likelihood that you will use them at the first opportunity. If you read just one hour per day, that will amount to about one book per week. One book per week will amount to about 50 books per year. Fifty books per year will total about 500 books over the next 10 years. At the very least, you will need a bigger house just to hold your books, and you will probably be able to afford it as well.

You have the opportunity this day to make it your greatest day ever. I guarantee you that the best day of your life is today. Today is your chance to become who you were designed to become. To do better and better. Show me a successful person that aimlessly gets out of bed and wonders out of this crazy world and succeeds at a higher level. They don't exist. Successful people are grateful people. Please stay away from too much social media news. There is enough time to try your brain for the rest of the day. Listen to me. What follow these two words 'I AM' will always come looking for you. You need to choose what follow the 'I AM'. When you go through the day saying 'I AM blessed, blessings come looking for you. When you say **I AM** talented, talent come looking for you. Stop asking people around you about their opinions about your belief. They may not even believe in your dream.

The most powerful words in your vocabulary are the words that you say to yourself and believe. Your self-talk, your inner dialogue, determines your emotions. Emotion is the key. The more intensely you desire a goal, the more rapidly it materializes. Combining your idea of your goal with the intense emotion of desire or excitement is like stepping on the accelerator of your mental potential. Your mind will speed up and generate ideas for goal accomplishment. The more positive, excited, and enthusiastic you are about achieving anything, the more rapidly your mind goes to work to bring it into your life.

Think about how you would feel if you had achieved your goal. Would you feel proud, happy, relieved, joyous, or euphoric? Whatever the emotion would be, you should confidently and happily imagine yourself enjoying the exact feeling that you would have if your goal were already a part of your life. If you want to earn more money and achieve a higher standard of living, imagine that you are already there, living the life you desire. Imagine how you would feel. Close your eyes and get the feeling of happiness, joy, and inner satisfaction. When you can combine a clear mental picture of your goal with the same emotion that you would have if it were achieved, you activate your higher powers of mind. You trigger your creativity. You get insights and ideas that will help you to achieve your goal far faster.

When you talk to yourself, your subconscious mind accepts these words as commands. It then adjusts your behavior, your self-image, and your body language to fit a pattern consistent with those words. From now on, talk to yourself only in terms of what you want to be and do. Refuse to say anything about yourself that you do not sincerely desire to be true. Repeat the powerful, positive words, "I can do it!" over and over. Prior to any occasion of importance, repeat the words, "I like myself!" Say, "I'm the best! I'm the best! I'm the best!" again and again like you really mean it. Then, stand up straight and strong, put a confident smile on your face, and do the very best of which you are capable. Soon it will become a habit.

Every change in your life will come about as the result of your mind colliding with a new idea. Ideas are the keys to the future. Ideas contain the answers to all of your problems and the ways to achieve all of your goals. Your need is to become an idea generator, so that you are continually coming up with new and better ideas to deal with the continuous changes and opportunities taking place around you. Fortunately, you are naturally creative. It is an innate quality. You are born with it. But creativity is subject to the Law of Use, which says, *"If you don't use it, you lose it,"* at least temporarily.

Each morning, after your daily reading, take a few minutes and rewrite your major goals in the present tense, exactly as if they already existed. Take a few seconds after rewriting each goal to visualize it as though it were already accomplished. See each goal in your mind as if it already existed. Then, smile, relax, and let go. This method of rewriting your goals each morning, visualizing them as if they had already been achieved, and then letting them go with complete confidence is a vital part of creating the mental equivalent of the things you want. By using this method, you will help your goals to materialize exactly when you are ready for them. By writing and rewriting your goals, you burn them deeper and deeper into your subconscious mind. At a certain point, you activate your superconscious mind. At that point, you begin attracting into your life people and circumstances that can help you to achieve them.

I hope you are enjoying the reading as I am right now. It is so good to read books like "Arise and Make a Difference; the Drive Behind Success". Can I please usher you to the next chapter, Dream Big Dreams? Alright let's go!

CHAPTER NINE

DREAM BIG DREAMS

"Get poisoned with your ever-increasing passion, dream, and zeal so that you can resurrect to become the world's best assert" (Vincent Lawer).

I got moved by the story of Joseph in the holy scripture. Joseph was an epitome of big dreamers. He dreamt yet another dream. He never stops dreaming until he finally fulfilled all those God-given dreams. My boss, never be deceived by the tiny dream you already have. Dream big. Dream bigger. And dream the biggest dream ever that existed on the planet earth.

You begin the process of becoming unstoppable by dreaming big dreams. Since everything you create in your world begins with a thought, the bigger the dreams you dream, the bigger the goals you will achieve. To realize your full potential, your greatest need is to break out of your limited thinking by dreaming big dreams and imagining unlimited possibilities. You need to remove all the negative beliefs that hold you back from becoming all you are capable of becoming.

All successful men and women are great dreamers. All topmost performers are what is called "blue-sky thinkers." They continually allow their minds to float freely when they think about what is possible for them. They look at the unlimited blue sky above them as the only limit to everything and anything that they could possibly be, or have or do. Give yourself permission to dream a lot bigger than "I'd like to get a Team Leader title, since I'm doing the job already" or "I'd be happy with a 6% increase." What would really make you happy, and how can you take a step toward the life you've designed for yourself? The more permission you give yourself to envision the life you want and deserve, the more easily you'll be able to see how to navigate there. A jerk boss is just a gnat buzzing around your head, if you are in charge of your career.

Permit me to ask you these questions; What one great thing would you dare to dream if you knew you could not fail? If you were absolutely guaranteed of success in the achievement of

> *"Don't ever lose your dream because you die the day you lose it."*
>
> *Samuel N. Adjovu*

any one goal, big or small, long-term or short-term, what would it be? If a billionaire took a liking to you and offered to write you a check to cover any goal that you could clearly define, what one goal would you choose? If you could have any job, what would it be? If you could work for any kind of company, what kind of a company would you select? Where would it be, and what would it be doing? If your family life and your relationships could be perfect in every respect, what would they look like? Good! Now answer these questions clearly. Write them down.

Successful people continually practice "back from the future" thinking. They project into the future several years and imagine what their lives would look like if they had achieved all of their goals. They look back to the present, from the mental vantage point of the future, like looking from the top of a high mountain down to where they are actually standing in the valley, in the present. They then look at the path that they would have to take to get to where they want to be in the future. Imagine your perfect lifestyle. If you had no limitations at all, how would you like to live, day in and day out? If you were financially independent, what kind of home would you like to live in? What kind of car would you want to drive? What kind of life would you like to provide for your family? What sort of activities would you like to engage in throughout the week, month, and year? How much time would you want to take off on vacation, and where would you like to go? What would you like to do? What sort of activities do you most enjoy?

If you were forced to take a month off from work and you had all the money you needed, how would you spend that time? Will you sleep through out? Success is an inside job. It is a state of mind. It begins within you and is soon reflected in the world around you. When you change your thinking for the better, you become a better person. By dreaming big dreams and envisioning an exciting future, you become a leader. By writing down your goals and making plans to accomplish them, you take full control of your life. And by practicing the ideas taught in this book, you can and will become unstoppable.

Arise and Make a Difference; the Drive Behind Success

By the law of correspondence, whatever you can clearly see on the inside, you will eventually experience on the outside. You should therefore envision your goals with as much clarity and vividness as possible. Visualize your goals intensely and create within yourself the same feeling that you would have if you had already achieved your goals. Envisage your goals frequently. Replay a picture of your goal, as if you had already realized it, on the screen of your mind as many times a day as you possibly can. Visualize your goals for *as* long as you possibly can, preferably just before falling asleep each night. Repeat these exercises of visualization; vividness, intensity, frequency, and duration; until your goals become absolutely clear, living, breathing, exciting, clear pictures in your mind. The more skilled you become at moving from the dream through the goal to the visualization, the more motivated and determined you will be. The more clarity you develop, the more courage and confidence you will have, and the more unstoppable

> *"Dream lofty dreams, and as you dream, so shall you become. Your vision is the promise of you shall at last unveil".*
> *John Ruskin*

you will become. Dreams without goals are just mere dreams and ultimately few disappointments. So, have dreams but have goals. The most significant part of dreaming big dreams is for you to define your *ideal future vision*. It is for you to think about what you want before you begin to think about what is possible for you. You dream big dreams by looking into the future and imagining that you have no limitations holding you back from achieving anything you set your mind on. Isolate yourself from your current situation and allow yourself to dream. Pretend for the moment that you have all the time and money you need. Imagine that you have all the connections and contacts, all the resources and opportunities, all the education and knowledge, all the skills and experience that you require to be, have, or do anything that you could dream of. Imagine your ideal lifestyle. Imagine your ideal job or income. Imagine where you would like to live and how you would like to spend each day, each week, each month. Imagine your ideal family life. Imagine your ideal state of health. Design your perfect life in every respect.

The starting point of great accomplishment is for you to break loose from the mental bonds that hold you back. Dreaming big dreams and setting big goals provide the starting point of thinking, seeing, and feeling yourself to be capable of achieving far more than you ever have before. How you think and feel about yourself is largely determined by how effective you feel you are in the important things you do, especially in your work or career. It is not possible for you to feel happy and confident as a person if you are not competent and capable in the areas of your life that are central to your personal identity. The truth is that the future belongs to the competent. You could lose all of your money tomorrow, but as long as you still had your ability to think and reason, you could make it all back and more besides. The future belongs to those who are better informed. The future belongs not to those who have more versus those who have less, but to those who know more versus those who know less.

One of the most powerful ways for you to change your thinking about yourself is for you to commit to excellence. It is to make the decision, right now, to be the best, to join the topmost in your field, no matter how long it takes. The very act of thinking of yourself as potentially excellent at what you do actually changes your mind-set and improves your personality. It makes you happier and raises your self-esteem. You like and respect yourself more, just by deciding to be the best.

Changing your thinking requires that you enlarge your ideas and imagination about the person you could be, the things you could do, and the things that you could have. Every person who accomplishes anything worthwhile in life begins with a big dream or a vision of what is possible for him or her. They rise above their current surroundings, their existing limitations and problems, and instead they imagine themselves sometime in the future living the kind of life they would like to live. You need to practice this way of thinking as well. Get the courage to dream big dreams. Dream dreams that the world cannot contain. Keep dreaming and fulfilling it until the world hear of you. Keep moving in the direction of bigger dreams. It is just a matter of time and all those dreams will be achieved.

It is very important to consider whose ears grabs your dream. That is what the next chapter of this book will elaborate. Now let's launched into the next chapter.

CHAPTER TEN

WHO HEARS YOUR DREAM?

"Some people want it to happen, some wish it would happen, others make it happen"
Michael Jordan

Welcome to a very important subtitle of this novel. It is very imperative that we critically read this subtitle and hence apply the result thereof. If dreams are what drive us to the accomplishment of our life long purpose in life in then it's very important to look at who we share our dreams with. It is one thing having a dream and another thing letting others hear of it. Whatever you tell others about your intentions has a strong determinant of the survival of your dream. What people hear about your dream can either sustain the dream or 'kill' the dream. Please allow me to draw you back to the bible a little, specifically in the old testament. Did you remember the story of Joseph? What was the reason why he was hated and tossed 'to' and 'fro' by his own brothers? Let me tell you the answer. The answer is very simple; he shared his dreams with his father and brothers. Joseph told them what God revealed to him in his dream.

In simple terms, the dreams of Joseph were interpreted that in future Joseph will rise up to rule over them all. Because of this they were all troubled and started plotting evil for him. In other words, they did not understand why their youngest brother who they were all other than will one day become their leader. Have you ever thought of yourself as the least in everything? Then I came to tell you that you are the next leader of your area. You are the next ruler of your family, community, church, in fact any organization you can think of. Hear me, be careful about what you share with others because they will make or unmake you. You can't trust anybody. No! not even your parents. Joseph trusted his father and therefore shared his dream with him but even his father was disturbed by the dream and got angry. Know and be sure of who hears your dream. If it is possible don't tell anybody about your dreams. Don't share with anybody your ideas.

Speak to your heavenly father to direct you in fulfilling that unique dream. Work on your dreams yourself. Don't be afraid to fail because nobody will help you. God is your ultimate help. Pray more to God to direct you and be focused on your dreams. Life is a box of rapped gift; you never know what you can get from it if not told by the giver. If you continue to work hard you will get what you want. Don't let small minds tell you that your dreams are too big. Surround yourself with people who see your value and remind you of it. Refuse to be understood by others. If everything about you makes sense to people then I can tell you that you are running below your speed limit.

Hear me! I didn't go to any media to broadcast my intension of writing this book you are reading now. In exception of my mentor, nobody, not even my parents knew about this tremendous move. I refuse to be predicted. If you really want to be a warrior of success then refuse to be predicted by your opponent. It is worthwhile of documenting your dream on paper than roaming about and broadcasting it with your mouth. For all you know someone is ready to steal that dream from you. Nurture that seed of vision in your mind and don't go ahead bragging about it. Keep it to yourself and only work hard at achieving it. Don't allow everything about you to be in the open to everyone's view. Give your life a password because so many people who don't have any ended nowhere. Refuse to be predicted by people. Don't let others know your next move in life. A true warrior is unpredictable because he dies the day his enemy predict him correctly.

CHAPTER ELEVEN

KNOW YOURSELF

"...for if you know better, you can do better."
Samuel N. Adjovu

The oldest of admonitions is **"Man, know thyself!"** If you market merchandise successfully, you must know the merchandise. The same is true in marketing yourself. You should know all of your weaknesses in order that you may either bridge them or eliminate them entirely. You should know your strength in order that you may call attention to it when selling your services. You can know yourself only through accurate analysis.

Knowledge of yourself can't be achieved if you don't understand the topic of self-concept. Why not relax and read this nugget of self-concept? Your self-concept has three elements, like a pie divided into three wedges. Each is linked with each of the others. All three elements together make up your personality. They largely determine what you think, feel, and do, and everything that happens to you.

Your *ideal-self* is the first part of your personality and your self-concept. Your ideal-self is made up of all of your hopes, dreams, visions, and ideals. Your self-ideal is composed of the virtues, values, and qualities that you most admire in yourself and others. Your ideal-self is the person you would most like to become, if you could be a perfect person in every way. For instance, you may like to become a Doctor, Police, President, Lawyer, Soldier, Nurse, Pastor, or any profession you can think of. These ideals guide and shape your behavior. Great men and women, leaders, and people of character are very clear about their values, visions, and ideals. They know who they are and what they believe in. They set high standards for themselves, and they don't compromise those standards. They are men and women that others can look up to and depend on. They are definite and distinct in their interactions with others. In everything they do, they strive to live up to their ideals.

The second part of your self-concept is your *self-image*. This is the way you see yourself and think about yourself. It is often called your "inner mirror." It is where you look internally to see how you should behave in a particular situation. Because of the power of your self-image, you always perform on the *outside* consistent with the picture you have of yourself on the *inside*. So, for instance, you may see yourself as a Doctor, Police, President, Lawyer, Soldier, Nurse, Pastor, or any profession you can think of. Don't forgot what I already said in the previous chapters that whatever you think of yourself that you become. Therefore, if you see yourself a Doctor, that you become. If you see yourself the President of this nation that you become. That is why you should never see yourself a failure. That is why you should never have negative thoughts about yourself. Think positively and become a positive thinker.

The third part of your self-concept is your *self-esteem*. This is the emotional component of your personality, and is the most important factor in determining how you think, feel, and behave. Your level of self-esteem largely determines much of what happens to you in life. Your self-esteem is best defined as *how much you like yourself.* The more you like yourself, the better you perform at anything you attempt. And by the law of reversibility, the better you perform, the more you like yourself. Your self-esteem is the "reactor core" of your personality. It is the energy source that determines your levels of confidence and enthusiasm. The more you like yourself, the higher will be the standards you will set for yourself. The more you like yourself, the bigger the goals you will set for yourself and the longer you will persist in achieving them. People with high self-esteem are virtually unstoppable.

Your level of self-esteem determines the quality of your relationships with others. The more you like and respect yourself, the more you like and respect others and the better they feel toward you. In your business life and career, your personal level of self-esteem will be the critical factor that determines whether or not people will buy from you, hire you, enter into business dealings with you, and even lend you money. The better your self-esteem, the better you will be as a spouse and parent. High self-esteem parents raise high self-esteem children. These children develop high levels of self-confidence and associate with other high self-esteem children. High self-esteem homes are characterized by love, laughter, and happiness for everyone who lives there.

The core of your personality is your level of self-esteem. Your self-esteem is a measure of how much you value yourself, and how much you think of yourself as an important and worthwhile person. Your self-esteem is the power source of your personality. It determines your levels of energy, enthusiasm, motivation, inspiration, and drive. The more you like and respect yourself, the better you do at everything you attempt. And the better you do, the more you like and respect yourself. Self-esteem and personal excellence reinforce each other.

To know yourself is your first priority! How can you realistically set goals, go about life and have successful relationships if you don't know who you are or what you want? You really can't. Not knowing yourself will lead to confusion and wasting much time in hit and miss situations. We tend to underestimate the importance of knowing ourselves. Many of us go through each day reacting to events and just getting by rather than making conscious choices based on who we are and what we want. When we don't know where we are headed it's hard to set goals, get motivated and determine the best course of action. Before we can do any of these things, we must establish who we are.

To know yourself:

- Be aware of your strengths, weaknesses, likes and dislikes
- Observe and be aware of your moods, reactions and responses to what is happening around you
- Become aware of how these moods and emotions affect your state of mind
- Examine how you interact with others
- Observe how your environment affects you

Knowing and understanding yourself better, in turn, leads to better decision making, setting and reaching appropriate goals and ultimately living more a productive life. There are many interesting personality tests and evaluations for self-discovery that can help you become more in tune to yourself and are also fun to do.

You can be different from the rest of the world and still be fabulous; in fact, you're fabulous *because of it*, not despite it. Different means good. So, if you are different, you, my dear, are good. The idea is to understand what makes you different, and as you do that, you get to know yourself better. It's perfectly fine to explore what your heart wants. It's completely alright to tune out the rest of the world so you can build a connection with your soul. It's remarkably uncommon, but it's fine and it's alright, so do it. You won't regret getting to know the person who lives inside you.

The most beautiful thing you will ever witness in your life is when you begin to unfold into the person you were meant to be from your very beginning. Knowing yourself is beyond figuring out your favorite color or your favorite subject in school or your favorite music album. We are no longer in high school; thank heavens where being "yourself" meant mimicking everyone else, acting stupid in the collective and defying rules, and feeling insecure all day long while doing it!

Knowing yourself is the process of understanding you; the human being on deeper levels than the surface. It is an unpredictable road that you must be *willing* to explore. It brings you face-to-face with your deep self-doubts and insecurities. It makes you take a serious look at the way you are living your life and put it to question. The whole thing can suck for a little while but then it gets better, and like anything else, a little hard work at the start pays dividends in abundance for the rest of your life.

Knowing yourself means respecting your values in life, your beliefs, your personality, your priorities, your moods, your habits, your magnificent body, and your relationships. Knowing yourself means understanding your strengths and weaknesses, your passions and fears, your desires and dreams. It means being aware of your eccentricities and idiosyncrasies, your likes and dislikes, and your tolerances and limitations. Knowing yourself means knowing your purpose in life. Or coming really darn close to finding it out!

You do not get to know yourself simply by growing up and growing old. Knowing yourself is a conscious effort; you do it with intention and purpose. Not knowing yourself becomes obvious sooner or later. A quiet frustration lives in your heart when you do not know yourself. You may choose to live with it and ignore it or you may choose to start getting to know yourself. Understanding your own personality is the first key. You have the collective opinion of others which is one aspect. You also have your own database of information about what your personality is really like, and who you are in your private moments as well as in your public ones.

The idea is to get to know your personality inside out, to know what you are and what you are not like. Understand what makes you react a certain way in life's myriad of situations. Ask yourself "Why did I do that?" and answer it. Who are you behind your name? What are your characteristic traits? Who are you among friends? What about strangers? What persona do you portray to the outside world? What are you really like on a good day as well as a bad day, in face of a challenge or a great reward? How do you react to the world around you?

Your core values are the morale codes and the principles you hold near and dear to your heart. When I work with my clients, one of the first things I ask prior to our coaching sessions is a list of their top eight core values. You probably have more than eight values, but the top eight play the big roles in decision-making, influencing, persuading, conflict-resolution, communication, and living your day-to-day life. In your work, in your home, in all aspects of your life, which values can you never compromise? Those are your core values. Is it honesty, integrity, security or flexibility? Is it dedication to others, wisdom and learning, financial comfort or fun? Do you value loyalty above excellence, responsibility above ambition, or innovation above improvement?

How well do you know your body, your breathing, your abilities, your limits of balance and flexibility? Have you ever said "my body can't do this" and that "my body type won't do that" without even trying a physical challenge? Before you close the door to wonderful possibilities, take another look. Take the time to become truly intimate with the loveliest temple on earth, your own body.

Your dreams and hopes create the pathway into your future. They help you build the life you can be proud of living. Your dreams matter. Your dreams are important. Your dreams are worth going after. Don't believe anything less. And start getting to know your dreams well. Get to know the details and the specifics. If you want to become a musician, ask yourself: What instrument do you want to play? What level of proficiency do you want to learn? How big a part of your life would it be? And on and on until you know everything about your dream. Make your dreams part of your daily pursuits. Take them seriously. Work at them. Glorify them instead of hiding them and being ashamed of them.

What do you like and just as important, what do you dislike? Simple, innocent question but knowing this about yourself gives you a lot of confidence into who you are. A lot of people go through life liking what's popular and disliking what's not "cool". Don't do that. Take the time to define your likes and dislikes, and don't put it up for a vote among family and friends. You decide. Defining your own likes and especially dislikes takes guts. It maybe impolite to dislike attending yet another baby shower or spending 3 hours with extended relatives, but look at the alternative. If you keep doing frustrates you and neglect what brings you joy, you give up part of who you are. It's the least likely path to any happiness whatsoever.

Stay true to your likes and dislikes. Nobody has to like them but you! Getting to know yourself allows you to tap into the well of happiness beyond your imagination. Bliss even on cloudy days. Start now to get to know yourself better today.

CHAPTER TWELVE

THE BURNING DESIRE

"What lies behind us, and what lies before us, are tiny matters compared to what lies within us."

-- Ralph Waldo Emerson

Your desire, which is the first step towards success must be a burning desire. Before you develop burning desire, you have to first understand what a burning desire is. This can be explained best in the following story:

Once upon a time, a young man wanted to know **how to have a burning desire** to achieve his goals, so he went to China to ask a wise Chinese man how to have strong and burning desire. The wise Chinese man got a large bowl of water and then put the young man's head in the bowl of water for a few minutes. The young man started slowly to get his head out of the water, but didn't succeed. After a few minutes, the young man shoved the wise Chinese man off and got his head out of the bowl of water. The young man asked, "What were you trying to do?" The wise Chinese man replied, "What did you learn from this experience?" The young man said, "Nothing." Then, the wise Chinese man replied, "Yes, you learned something. At first, when you tried to get your head out of the bowl of water, you weren't successful because your desire was not strong enough, but after words when your desire was strong, you were able to get your head out of the bowl of water and this is exactly the type of desire needed to achieve one's goal."

You may probably want to answer this question for me; Do you have strong and burning desire to achieve your goals? Do you have a burning desire to get up in the morning to do everything it takes to make your goal a reality? This is an imperative question that you have to answer. Many people say they want something and after a while they lose interest. Why? It is because they don't know the real reason why they want this specific goal. Why do you want your goal? Does it give you freedom? Stability? Security? Without strong, burning desire and will power, you will give up quickly, you will not persist and hence you won't achieve what you had in mind. Knowing exactly why you want something, helps keep the burning desire awake inside of you at all times and it will lead you to take action.

Thomas visualized a Edison lamp that could be operated by electricity, began where he stood to put his dream into action, and despite more than ten thousand failures, he stood by that dream until he made it a physical reality. Practical dreamers **Do Not Quit!** The Wright brothers dreamed of a machine that would fly through the air. Now one may see evidence all over the world that they dreamed soundly. The world has become

> *"In order to succeed your desire to succeed must be greater than your fear of failure"*
> **Bill Cosby**

accustomed to new discoveries, and it has shown a willingness to reward the dreamer who gives the world a new idea. The greatest achievement was, at first, and for a time, but a dream. The oak sleeps in the acorn. The bird waits in the egg, and in the highest vision of the soul, a waking angel stirs. **Dreams are the seedlings of reality**. Awake, arise, and assert yourself, you dreamers of the world.

Your star is now in the ascendency. The world is filled with an abundance of opportunity which the dreamers of the past never knew. A burning desire to be, and to do is the starting point from which the dreamer must take off. Dreams are not born of indifference, laziness, or lack of ambition. The world no longer makes fun at the dreamer, nor calls him impractical. Remember, too, that all who succeed in life get off to a bad start, and pass through many heartbreaking struggles before they "arrive." The turning point in the lives of those who succeed usually comes at the moment of some crisis, through which they are introduced to their "other selves."

Edison, the world's greatest inventor and scientist, was a "tramp" telegraph operator. He failed countless times before he was driven, finally, to the discovery of the genius which slept within his brain. Charles Dickens began by pasting labels on blacking pots. The catastrophe of his first love pierced the nadirs of his soul, and changed him into one of the world's truly great authors. That catastrophe produced, first, David Copperfield, then a succession of other works that made this a richer and better world for all who read his books.

Helen Keller became deaf, dumb, and blind shortly after birth. Despite her greatest misfortune, she has written her name indelibly in the pages of the history of the great. Her entire life has served as evidence that no one ever is defeated until defeat has been accepted as a reality. Booker T. Washington was born in slavery, handicapped by race and color. Because he was tolerant, had an open mind at all times, on all subjects, and was a **dreamer**, he left his impress for good on an entire race. I feel like shouting now because something is burning inside me right now that I wish to echo in your ears again that there is more place for you at the top. I challenge you to rise up now make a tremendous difference in this life.

Beethoven was deaf, Milton was blind, but their names will last as long as time endures, because they dreamed and translated their dreams into organized thought. Dr. Mae Jemison was the first African-American woman to travel into space. From her humble beginning to space was no small achievement. Light in your mind the fire of hope, faith, courage, and tolerance. If you have these states of mind, and a working knowledge of the principles described, everything you need will come to you, when you are ready for it.

Ideas are intangible forces, but they have more power than the physical brains that give birth to them. They have the power to live on, after the brain that creates them has returned to dust. For example, take the power of Christianity. That began with a simple idea, born in the brain of Christ. Its chief precept was, "Do unto others as you would have others do unto you." Christ has gone back to the source from whence He came, but His idea goes funneling on. Someday, it may grow up, and come into its own, then it will have fulfilled Christ's deepest desire. The idea has been developing only two thousand years. Give it time! Success requires no explanations; failure permits no explanations.

You were born to shape the world. You are a star created to illuminate so go ahead and light the world with your star. Let your hunger for success push you pass the pressures and pain that demands your halt from being the change that the world awaits. You possess a story that must be written for generations to come. If you really want to live your dream, you've got to burn your ship and burn that thing that makes it easier for you to retreat. If you can clearly see where you are going, you shall soon get there. If you can clearly see it you can have it.

Plan your future! Plan the way you want your future to be like. The most intelligent man living cannot succeed in accumulating money nor in any other undertaking; without plans which are practical and workable. Just keep this fact in mind, and remember when your plans fail, that temporary defeat is not permanent failure. It may only mean that your plans have not been sound. Build other plans. Start all over again. Thomas A. Edison "failed" ten thousand times before he perfected the incandescent electric light bulb. That is, he met with temporary defeat ten thousand times, before his efforts were crowned with success.

Temporary defeat should mean only one thing; the certain knowledge that there is something wrong with your plan. Lots of men go through life in misery and poverty because they lack a comprehensive plan through which to amass a fortune. Get out of the comfort zone and march boldly into the door ahead of you and if it closes, remember closed doors are the reasons your hands are in shape. So, push it open. Henry Ford accumulated a fortune, not because of his superior mind, but because he adopted and followed a plan which proved to be sound. A thousand men could be pointed out, each with a better education than Ford's, yet each of whom lives in poverty, because he does not possess the plan for the accrual of money. Your achievement can be no greater than your plans are sound. That may seem to be an axiomatic statement, but it is true.

There can be no compromise between poverty and riches! The two roads that lead to poverty and riches travel in opposite directions. If you want riches, you must refuse to accept any circumstance that leads toward poverty. The word "riches" is here used in its broadest sense, meaning financial, spiritual, mental and material estates. The starting point of the path that leads to riches is desire.

Anybody can wish for riches, and most people do, but only a few know that a definite plan, plus a burning desire for wealth, are the only dependable means of accumulating wealth. Life is such that you'd wish carry the cross others but the rules don't permit it. Nobody can succeed for you. You must do it all by yourself.

CHAPTER THIRTEEN

DEVELOP YOUR RESOURCES

"If you go to work on your goals, your goals will go to work on you. If you go to work on your plan, your plan will go to work on you. Whatever good things we build end up building us."

-- Jim Rohn

Most of us are like wild land; undeveloped. We show signs of real wealth, but it is lying underneath the roots and stumps and refuse that need to be cleared away to make the soil usable. Here is a voice with marvelous timbre, but no training. They wrote across it, "Unusable, undeveloped." Here is a face with a smile that has been enveloped up in it a fortune, but the mind back of it is untrained, inept, unready. We write across it, "Unavailable." What we need is hard work, not work on impulse, but on principle. We need to drive ourselves until we have developed the rich resources within us. The time to do it is now.

Begin today to clean up that rich bottom land in your nature, and get it into production at once. Make everything swing into line now to the one great objective of your life. Determine your future; settle what you are going to do and then make every day pay tribute. Transform it into vital energy. Set the turbine of a tremendous purpose loose inside of you. Indecision and wastefulness of ability and time must be destroyed. Fight for time. It is the most valuable asset you have. Cut every corner. Save every moment.

Be exact with yourself. Put yourself on a schedule. Make yourself do your best. Wasting time is wasting ability. It is wasting the thing that makes you worthwhile. Learn to use it. Make your time your wealth. Make moments pay dividends. Carve out of every day that which spells success for tomorrow. Make yourself worthwhile. Make people want you. Make yourself so attractive, so vitally attractive, so valuable that men will hunt after you. Make opportunities where no opportunities ever existed before. Make yourself ready for the opportunity. Don't settle for less because there are priceless treasures within you that you have no idea of.

Take some risk because the greatest loss of warrior is the risk of not taking a risk. The earth has opportunities for you, and they appear in different forms. Some from obscure directions that you least expect them. Opportunities always appear in mask. More often than not, many opportunities come disguised in the form of misfortune or temporary breakdown. But you need to see beyond all that. Hear me! Where you are going is worth more than what you are going through. And what you've been through already is the benchmark of your stamina for breakthrough. You are in a serious catastrophe if you think other people are responsible where you are. You are heading for doom if you ever think your financial independence lies in the hand of an employer. You are the conductor of your vehicle and you decides where to drive to.

Here me, money is as shy and elusive as the "old time" maiden. It must be wooed and won by methods not unlike those used by a determined lover, in pursuit of the girl of his choice. And, coincidental as it is, the power used in the "wooing" of money is not greatly different from that used in wooing a maiden. That power, when successfully used in the pursuit of money must be mixed with faith. it must be mixed with desire. It must be mixed with persistence. It must be applied through a plan, and that plan must be set into action. Don't permit the world to amaze you, rather be the amazing episode ever recorded in the pages of the world.

When money comes in quantities known as "the big money," it flows to the one who accumulates it as easily as water flows downhill. There exists a great unseen stream of power, which may be compared to a river; except that one side flows in one direction, carrying all who get into that side of the stream, onward and upward to wealth. The other side flows in the opposite direction, carrying all who are unfortunate enough to get into it (and not able to extricate themselves from it), downward to misery and poverty. I can see abundance of wealth inside you now. Rise up and develop those resources and make a big difference that will be written in the minds of many generations to come.

Invest first in education. In reality, the only real asset you have is your mind, the most powerful tool we have dominion over. Each of us has the choice of what we put in our brain once we're old enough. You can watch TV, read educative magazines, or go to ceramics class or a class on financial planning. You choose. Most people simply buy investments rather than first investing in learning about investing. Develop your intelligence. A truly intelligent person welcomes new ideas, for new ideas can add to the synergy of other accumulated ideas. Listening is more important than talking. If that were not true, God would not have given us two ears and only one mouth. Too many people think with their mouth instead of listening in order to absorb new ideas and possibilities. They argue instead of asking questions.

Often people ask about the role of *luck* in success. They are convinced that luck is a critical factor in achieving anything worthwhile. They feel that some people are just lucky and some are not. They talk about luck as if it were a matter of fate or destiny, largely inexplicable. They insist that a person gets to the top of his field largely as the result of getting lucky breaks, which they, of course, did not get. Luck is a word that people use to explain away things that turn out much better than could have been expected. If a person achieves great financial success at a young age, people say he was "just lucky." Some people use luck to describe something remarkably good that happens that is out of the ordinary. But it is not luck at all. The fact is that all so-called lucky outcomes are really the result of *probabilities*. There is no such thing as luck. The Law of Probabilities says that there is a probability for everything that happens. Listen to me my boss, even if there is any word as luck then now is the time for you to rise up and create your own luck.

To make a huge difference in life, you've got to stop wasting the resource none as 'time'. Brain Tracy, in his book; *'Richness and Success'* made an imperative statistic. He said, "the average employed person puts in about 40 hours per week on the job, but only about 32 hours of that is officially working time. Fully 50 percent of time spent at work is wasted in idle socializing with co-workers, personal telephone calls, and personal business. Average employees start a little later, take long coffee breaks and lunch hours, and leave a little earlier. Even managers privately report that they spend fully half of the time they are at work doing things that have absolutely nothing whatever to do with the job. Only about 5 percent of people working today work full-time on their jobs from the time they begin each day until the time they finish. These people are the ones on the fast track in their careers. They are moving upward and onward, getting paid more and being promoted faster. They are the movers and shakers in every business, and everyone knows who they are. My boss, it's time to rise up and develop your resources because that is the road to an unfathomable success.

Most people refuse to develop their human resource. This is the cause of the rampant downsizing that developing countries are currently experiencing. Every year, hundreds of thousands of people are laid off from large and small corporations, often from white-collar jobs. Why is this? The answer is simple. The companies have finally learned that they are paying high salaries to people who are producing very little of value. No company can survive very long under these conditions, and these companies are determined to survive. So, the redundant staff has to go.

You've got to utilize your time very well if you really want to make a difference and become successful. Go beyond the normal time of closing work. I always come to work early but closes late. This novel you have in your hand now came to being due to the extra time I spent in office after everyone closed from work. Go for an extra time and develop your abilities. The idea of the five-day week, which was promoted by the labor unions as a great advance in the life of the working person, has been the cause of more financial underachievement and failure than perhaps any other single myth. The fact is that, especially at the beginning of their careers, all really successful people work much harder than the average person. They work 10 to 12 hours per day, six days per week. They work at this rate for many months and years, before they reach the point where they can slow down. The average self-made millionaire has taken 22 years to get from being broke to having a net worth of more than one million dollars. It is not easy and it is not quick. But it is definitely possible if you want it badly enough.

Napoleon Hill, the author of *Think and Grow Rich*, once told the story of a young man who started at the bottom of a large organization and eventually moved up into the top ranks of executives, passing all the people who had started with him at the same level. His strategy was simple. He noticed that his boss came in a little earlier than the rest of the staff, stayed to finish up his work, and left a little later than the others. This young man therefore resolved to arrive 15 minutes before his boss and to leave 15 minutes after his boss left. He put his resolution into action the next day. This is another hallmark of high achievers: They don't procrastinate when they have a good idea; they take action immediately. The young man began coming in 15 minutes before his boss and going straight to work, continuing all day. When his boss left, he would still be at his desk, working away.

The boss said nothing for several weeks. Finally, after work one evening, his boss came over to his desk and asked him why he always seemed to be there, even though all his co-workers had left. The young man said it was because he was really determined to be successful in this company, and he knew he couldn't be successful unless he was willing to work harder than anyone else. The boss smiled and nodded and went on his way. Soon after that, the boss asked him to do something that was not part of his job description. He did it quickly and well, delivered it to his boss, and went back to his desk. Soon after, he was given another assignment, which he also completed quickly. Within a year, the young man had been given several additional responsibilities, each one of which he accepted and fulfilled immediately.

In his second year, he was promoted to a higher position. He studied, upgraded his skills, and continued to work hard. Within a couple of years, he had surpassed all of his rivals. He had earned the respect and esteem of the other managers. They soon promoted him so that he was one of them, rather than one of the staffs. His career took off. Eventually he became a vice president of the company. This is a simple strategy that works for anyone who is willing to do more than is expected of him or her. It works for almost anyone, anywhere, over and over again, year after year. This is what I need you to do after reading this book. Go out there and work hard. Don't be that indolent man or woman I know. That's not your potion!

You may think that you lack the education, opportunities, or resources that other successful people seem to have. Don't worry. The fact is that most people start off with few advantages. The story of most successful people is the story of people who started with nothing and did something worthwhile with their lives. Most people try and fail at a lot of things before they find the right situation for their talents and abilities. The fact is that everything you ever achieve you are going to have to do it *yourself*. No one is going to do it for you. But if you keep learning and growing, trying lots of things, you will eventually get the breaks. Everyone does. Just remember that opportunities are like a fumble in a football game. If you don't personally pick up the ball and run with it, it just lies there and has no effect on the score. When you get your chance, take action on it immediately.

The biggest mistake that you can make is to think that you ever work for anyone else but yourself. The fact is that you are always self-employed, from the time you take your first job until the time you retire. No matter who signs your paycheck, you are working for *yourself*. You are the president of an entrepreneurial personal services company with one employee; *yourself*. In the long run, as a result of the things that you do or fail to do, you determine how much you earn. If you want an increase in pay, you can go to the nearest mirror and negotiate with your "boss."

Seeing yourself as the president of your own personal services corporation requires that you accept total responsibility for everything you are, and everything you ever will be. This is an enormous thought for many people. It is both scary and exhilarating. Just imagine! You are where you are and what you are because you have decided to be there. Everything you accomplish, for the rest of your life, will be largely determined by the actions that you take, or fail to take. You are responsible. You are in charge. You are in control. You are your own boss. And there are no limits except the limits that you allow the outside world to place on yourself and on your thinking.

Hear me my boss, if you really need to develop your resources then don't ignore mentors in your journey of making a difference. Most successful people have mentors at different stages of their lives. A person whom you know and who knows you and helps you on a regular basis often determines your success in life. The right mentor at the right time can save you from countless mistakes and years of hard work. My interest in writing wasn't just about me, but rather I was inspired by mentors. Many people are a little bit fuzzy about exactly how mentoring relationships work. A mentor is like an uncle. He or she is an older friend, someone wiser and more experienced than you, who will give you guidance and advice from time to time. A mentor can help you avoid pitfalls that might sidetrack your career or hold you back.

At each stage of your life you can benefit from the advice and experience of someone who is further along the path than you. The men who have been there to give me guidance and advice as I grew up and gone into writing at various levels have affected my life dramatically. This type of relationship can have a major impact on your success as well. The primary source of value today is not land, labor, and other hard assets, but knowledge, information, and ideas. The greatest treasure you could possibly possess is between your ears. You can make an unlimited future for yourself by tapping into your brainpower and channeling it, like a powerful current, to energize your life and get you anything you really want.

Hear me! The primary source of value today is *knowledge*. Since there is no boundary to the amount of knowledge you can acquire, there is no boundary to the amount of value that you can create. You can start from wherever you are, no matter what your background, and begin to increase your mental assets. You can start work today on improving your ability to perform and get results for which others will pay. The wonderful thing about knowledge is that it can be reproduced hundreds of thousands, even millions of times without losing its value. It is the one commodity that can actually be infinite in its application. If you or someone else comes up with a new idea to do something faster or better, that idea can be spread around the world in no time at all, and be in the hands of millions of other people who can also use it to improve their lives and work just like you have this piece of writing in your hands. And you have lost nothing. The idea still has its original value to you. This is absolutely incredible.

The most successful people today are those who are continually investing in learning and expanding their intellectual asset base. They are wide open to new ideas and new approaches. A major mistake made by many people, especially those who have graduated from a university, is that they conclude that everything they know at the moment is all that they need to know about a particular subject. Sometimes they think that what they know is all they *need* to know about a subject as well. This is called the "intelligence trap" of the poor performer, the *unconscious incompetent*. This is a person who does not know, and does not know that he does not know. This person cannot be helped, because he is closed to new information. This is why the beginning of all wisdom is often the awareness of how ignorant you really are, of how little you really know.

Develop your level of creativity. Creativity is your inheritance. You are a highly intelligent individual with a continuous flow of good ideas that you can use to accomplish goals and improve your life. In fact, even if you have not used your creativity for a long time, and most people have not, you can stir it up, like sugar that has sunk to the bottom of a cup of coffee. There is a Law of Probabilities that applies to creative thinking and tapping into the powers of your mind. This law says that *the more ideas that you are exposed to, the more likely it is that you will be exposed to the right idea, exactly when you need it.* The most successful people today are those who are constantly exposing themselves to new ideas from a variety of sources. Unsuccessful people, in contrast, are those who continue to recirculate the same worn-out old ideas with little imagination or creativity.

When you attend a seminar or a lecture given by an expert who is sharing some of the most current ideas in his or her field, you will often receive a bombardment of new insights that you can use to improve parts of your life. Many people's lives have been completely changed as the result of attending a single lecture given by a single intelligent person who gave them a single insight that was the key to their future. Imagine what would happen if you attended courses, seminars, and lectures on a regular basis. You would be continually bombarding your mind with new ideas that would keep your mind alert and aware, and keep your creative juices flowing. If you are really in the same boat with me of making a difference and becoming successful in life then you've got to be more creative like never before.

Creative people are constantly reading, not only in their own fields but in other fields as well. They read primarily nonfiction. They subscribe to a variety of magazines and newspapers. They are continually scanning through the tables of contents and through the critical articles. Always read with a pen or highlighter in your hand. Even better, learn how to speed-read so that you can scan material at a thousand words a minute, or faster. Speed-reading is a skill, like driving a car, that anyone can learn with a few hours of application. Forever after, you will be able to process more information than perhaps you ever imagined possible.

Develop your resources by befriending creative and intelligent people. Effective people make a habit of associating with other positive, creative people. They are constantly sharing ideas and experiences, learning from each other. They cut clippings out of magazines and newsletters, and pass them on to their friends. They recommend books they have read and audio programs they have listened to. Their friends do the same for them. Sometimes one good idea that you get from someone else can change the direction of your life.

It's been exciting coming this far. Congratulations! Having read extensively on developing your resources, lets us now launch into the next chapter; Abilities Count.

CHAPTER FOURTEEN

ABILITIES COUNT

What Do You Have in Yourself? It is what you are, what you have in you that counts. It is the undeveloped resources in your mind, in your spirit, in that inward man that counts. It is the developing of the writer, the thinker, the teacher, the inventor, the leader, the business manager that is hidden deep in you that is important. I am very optimistic that every one of you young men and women who read this have in you one of these abilities. There may be an untrained voice, untrained musical abilities lying hidden under the careless, thoughtless exterior.

Let us go down with a flashlight and look over the untouched treasures that are stored away inside, that have never been touched, never been used. Then let us bring the thing up that we find and make it worthwhile; give it a commercial value. For remember that everything that goes toward making you a success is inside of you. The thing that makes opportunities, that makes money, that saves money, that creates new things, that brings together things that others have created but were unable to utilize, is inside of you. Find it and make it work. It is going to require a boss who is utterly heartless to rule over you. The boss is inside of you.

There is a slave driver in there whom you must bring out. Put the whip in his hand and tell him to go to it and make you a success. There is something in you that can take these dreams of yours and make blue prints of them, and then can change the blue prints into buildings. It is there. That ability is there. No one else can train it. No one else can develop it. Someone else may set it on fire, but you can quench the fire by refusing to act. Remember that you must use the suggestions that come; you must rise up and put the thing over. You must drive yourself, for no one else can do it. Put yourself on a mental diet, not a diet of idle dreams nor idle fancies, but a diet of real mental work. Be mentally awake, diligent. Put your best into every day. Make up your day of saved moments, hours. You are out to win. You are out to conquer. You can do it! It would be different if this ability were in someone else and you were trying to awaken it. It is all in you and you are going to put it over. It is one thing having an ability and another thing utilizing that ability. Just possessing an ability without using it does not guarantee your success in life left alone making a difference.

Let me tell you something, there is a gold mine hidden in every life. Find out what you wish to be or do, then train yourself for it. What you have not developed in you has no value. No one else either wishes or has the time to develop it. That is your business. The training is all done by you. If you have a voice, put yourself under a teacher; then work and carry out the teacher's instructions. If it is art, put yourself under a competent instructor and obey the laws of art and work. If it is about sports, discipline yourself under the supervision of a coach. Nothing will take the place of hard work, intelligently directed. Talents in you need push and determination to make them worth money. It is you, and you alone, who will do the developing. The lazy person who waits for something to turn up is a failure. The only things that will turn up are rent and bills.

I remembered vividly what Prof. Ahiatrogah, a Professor at the University of Cape Coast (UCC) said when he was lecturing BSc. Psychology level 300 students in a course called Psychology of Adulthood. He said, "Don't form the habit of passing by or visiting every lecturer in their offices with the intent of greeting them. In fact, what has greeting lecturers have to do with your future prospect of life?" It's time to showcase your adult ability. Look for the possibilities available. Yes, I mean it. Possibilities are available all over. This nation has no employment for you after school. Create that opportunity you have been dreaming about and be independent.

Gone were the days when our educational elite attended school for free and ended up securing an employment immediately after completion. In fact, companies and organizations were waiting for them on their various campuses to select them immediately they were done with their last final examinations. In our time nothing of that privilege exist. You have to fight for it. Don't quit until you get it all. Get up young man or woman and wipe the sleep off your face because those days of working for the government or any company all your life and go home finally after sixty years with a little pension token are far gone. Always try to climb to the top of your life because the bottom is overcrowded and has no space for an intelligent person like you. The top has more rooms prepared for you, therefore yearn for the top.

Nothing will take the place of self-denial and hard work. It is easy to become a failure; all you need to do is to idly dream. It is the man who wills and keeps on willing who wins. Don't float. Don't wait for an opportunity. Go make your opportunity. Put your whole self into life. Study, drive yourself. Always remember that your worst enemy is inside of you. No circumstance, no person or combination of persons can conquer you as long as you do not destroy your own prospects yourself. Don't be satisfied with anything you do. Always seek to improve yourself. Nature never made anyone a failure. Every man has success hidden away in his soul. No one else can find yours but yourself. You hold the key to the hidden room. Failure comes because we never sought that hidden treasure. Failure comes because we tried to find it somewhere else. You can't find it anywhere else.

Success, victory, and achievement is in you. The exceptional people are those who develop what is within them. That quartet is winning fame and success because they developed what they had in them. Singly they could not do it but united they make a harmony that thrills the heart. The pianist had it in him. It was there and he developed it and made it of commercial value. E. W. Kenyon, the author of *'Sign-Posts on the Road to Success'* gave a about three great baritones. One was a miner who, had he not been too lazy and loved the companionship of drinking men and useless women, would have been known the world over.

"What a voice he had. I picked him up a drunkard. I tried to make a man of him. I bought him clothes. When it was known that Scotty was going to sing, the building could not hold the crowd. I said to him, I don't know whether my pianist can play the pieces that you want to sing without looking them over. He looked at me with a peculiar expression and said, 'I need no accompaniment.' He stood by the piano that first night in his old mining clothes and sang. I closed my eyes and I couldn't locate him because his voice utterly filled that whole room. He seemed to be everywhere in it.

That great voice was strange, sweet, wonderful music. He made the songs all over that he sang that night. I raised the money and sent him back to his own land. He promised to sing again. As a boy he sang in Drewry but he confessed he was so drunk that it took a man to hold him up. But he never amounted to anything. He did not develop the thing that was in him'. Genius have grown up to weeds about it, just because they did not develop the thing they have. I know it is hard work but you will learn to love hard work. There are no great gold nuggets lying on top of the earth now. You have to go down into the earth for them; you must dig for them. You want the applause of the world? You want money to buy fine clothes and build splendid houses? Awake young man! Go find that hidden place in your own nature. Dig and dig until you have conquered.

A father was dying. He had two sons. The boys had always felt that he had gold that he had hidden away somewhere. He had never been a strong, healthy man so his farm was not developed. Back of the house there was ten acres of stump land. When he was dying, he said, "The stump lot." Again, and again he said, "The stump lot." As soon as the funeral was over the boys said, "The gold is out in the stump lot." How feverishly they worked. They tore up every inch of it. But they found no gold. Then the older one said, "We have the land in good condition, let's put in corn." In the autumn they found in the ripened corn the gold. You have a stump lot in you. Dig it up, clean it up, and you will find the gold in it. There is room and a salary waiting for the man who has ability and is willing to put hard work into it. Submit yourself to more education. Education is primarily the key to success. Keep investing into education because I can see you reaping bountifully from it soon. I know few educated people whose one day sitting allowances for a short meeting is four times more than five years annual salary of some workers. Why is it so? Because they invested more into educating themselves so that the world will pay them for their little services.

Choose your work, rather than have the work in which you have no interest thrust upon you. Find out what you can do, what you like best to do. I don't care who you are. I don't care what your handicaps are. They have never made a handicap that could hold any man down who had in him the yeast to rise. Most of the people who are at the bottom are at the bottom because they will to stay there. That is where they belong. It is a hard thing to say, but it is true. I am now what I willed to be through all these years. The first thing to do is to find out what you want. Set your eyes on the goal. Then fight for it. There must be an objective. When you find that objective, set your compass and sail for that star.

The preliminary point of identifying your special talents and unique abilities is for you to think back into your past. What sorts of activities have given you your greatest results and rewards? When you were in school, what subjects interested you the most? What subjects did you get the best grades in? You will always be best at doing something that attracts you, that holds your attention, that captures your interest, and that you are naturally attracted toward. One of the tests for whether something is right for you is your desire to learn more about it. You will enjoy reading about it, talking about it, and learning about it. Not only that, but you will naturally admire the people who are the most successful in the field for which you are ideally suited. Napoleon Hill once said that one of the great secrets of success is to *decide what it is that you most enjoy doing, and then find a way to earn a good living at it*. Most people get it backward. They do what they feel they *have to do* so that they can finally acquire the time and money necessary to do what they really *want to do*. Your goal should be to reverse this order.

You should do what you really enjoy doing from the very beginning. In this way, you will get better and better doing more and more of the things that give you your greatest feeling of importance. Many of the happiest men and women in our society today are those who, at a certain point, got up and walked away from a situation that they finally realized was not making them happy or fulfilled. They had the courage to decide that they were going to do what they loved to do, rather than what they felt they had to do. They looked deep within themselves and honestly assessed their own natural talents and abilities. This often changed their whole lives.

Great success and happiness come when you identify your natural abilities, and then concentrate on developing along the lines of your inborn talents. It is almost as though you are engineered for success in a specific way, and if you can find the area for which you were specifically designed, you will achieve more in a few years than most people achieve in a lifetime. Please don't leave anything to chance. You don't hope for miracles or wish for a lucky break. You must recognize that if it's to be, it's up to you.

Since you know you are going to have to spend the rest of your life working at something, you must decide in advance that you will do what you love to do. You will become everything you are capable of becoming by developing your unique talents and abilities, wherever they lead. You will work only at something you enjoy, with people you enjoy, doing work that makes a difference in the world. You must set high standards for yourself. You must always think positively and constructively about your career and your future. You must recognize that anything that anyone else has done you can do as well and even better. Once you have decided what it is you want to do, you must throw your whole heart into doing it in an excellent fashion. And as a result, you become unstoppable.

I am so privileged to have led you through this inspirational journey. Stay calm and enjoy the next and very exciting mind-blowing chapter.

CHAPTER FIFTEEN

THE LION ATTITUDE

"Nothing can stop the man with the right mental attitude from achieving his goal; nothing on earth can help the man with the wrong mental attitude."

-- Thomas Jefferson

Sheep follow a leader and a herd. They don't know where they're going. Many times, they are led to the slaughter house but they keep following. They don't lead. They don't use their mind. A lion leads. It's about having the courage to stand and fight for your life. Having the strength to go bravely, to go in your own direction even if others walk away. You tread your own path because only you know what is best for you. Only you know the path to take. Only you know your courage, strength, and heart. Everyone has a heart of a lion inside them. It's no fan that the scripture describes us the lion of Judah. Now let that lion out! Let it scream out of you like a hungry lion. Unleash the beast inside you. Attitude is what you think, do, and feel about yourself. Your attitudes, positive or negative, constructive or destructive, lead to corresponding images, emotions, and actions that affect your life and relationships. Your attitudes, in turn, are based on your previous experiences and your basic premises about how things are supposed to be.

Attitude is everything in life. Guess why? Whether you rise or fall, all is based on the attitude that you showed at that moment. "Your attitude they say determine your altitude ". Maintain a positive attitude at all times. Never leave your mind opened to the negative thoughts and conditioning of others. Your positive attitude will help your destiny. Listen carefully, I've been through hard times. I've experienced it and I want you to know that it wasn't my money that brought me this far. It was my attitude towards life. It was my attitude to keep going when the going got tough. That's is the lion attitude I am talking about. The good question to ask you at this juncture is what is your attitude towards life? What do you think of yourself as I am talking to you now? So, do you think of yourself as God thinks of you or you think of yourself as how friends and family members think of you?

My dear, you need the lion attitude. The attitude to take charge of your destiny. You need the lion attitude that says "1 can". You need that lion attitude that says "I will" because I am bold enough to fight. You need the lion attitude if you are standing in for GREATNESS. Real lions are hungry when the time comes for their mission. Lions are not and will never be followers even at their weakest moment. They are the leaders that lead the rest of the animals. Become a lion now! Be fearless! Don't just talk; walk the talk. Real lions demonstrate who they are. Hear me, a lion does not seek for respect. They command respect and authority because they know they should be respected. Be a lion but not a sheep because a sheep

> *No one pities a lion. He is the king of the jungle and doesn't need anyone to feel sorry for it.*

follows a leader. A lion leads! I repeat "it's about having the courage to stand and fight for your life". Having the strength to go in your own direction even if no one believes in you. Don't fit in. Stand out and use your gift.

Don't be jealous of the successful because the world is changing every second so fast that the first may become the last and the last may become the first. The lion is certain. There are no " maybes" with the lion. "This is my decision and I will attack until the outcome is mine". No one will push me around. No one will tell me where to go or what to do. If I want something, I will go for it with everything I have inside me! The sheep is not certain that is why they follow a herd. Not knowing where they are going. Not meticulous, just drifting through life, being pulled and peddled. Being shred from head to toe until there is nothing left to give out and that's what I see in some people.

Refuse to be those people! Life, the world, and society is shredding you of your very self. Head to toe you lose your own unique footprint. You become what others want you to see not what you want to be. Once again don't let anyone push you around. Be like a lion! Roar so loud with your own spirit that no one will doubt you ever again. No one will question your goals. No one will dare challenge you again because you certainly will shine through like a lion. An army of sheep led by a lion will always defeat an army of lions led by a sheep.

The lion is my favorite animal. Maybe because it just follows its instincts and does what he wants. The lion is the prime example of the alpha male. It's the alpha animal of the jungle. The king of the jungle is also the most alpha animal there is. Size does not matter in the jungle otherwise the elephant would have been the king of the jungle. It's all about the mindset over there. Only the strongest survive. This also applicable to our modern society. Therefore, only the people of the strongest mindset (the lions) will get the most out of life, all the others (the sheep) will follow. The most imperative attribute of the lion is that 'everybody can do it'. Animals can't change their attitude but we humans can make the change. We can become a lion and adopt the lion attitude.

Don't be mentally weak and soft! Tell yourself the truth because until you do it, you will remain an average complaining hater like the majority of the people around you are. You will be bitter for the rest of your life because you will be regretting why you never stood for what you believed in. Refuse to be pulled and trudged like the sheep. Refuse to be sheared from head to toes until there is nothing left to give. Refuse to be like the majority of the people who are allowing the world and the society to shear them from head to toes till they lose their unique footprint! If you want to stand out like a lion, then you have to refuse to be pushed around like the majority of the people.

Leadership begins with self-discovery. It begins when you realize that you can become better than you already are. It grows when you have the courage to defend your beliefs even if every other person is against you. It rises when you refuse to fit in because you do not like what your friends are doing anymore! A person with the lion attitude thinks positively about himself. He believes that he can achieve anything that he sets out to do. He is disciplined to stay on course even when the obstacles become many. He does not believe what others say of his abilities because he knows that there are no limitations to what he can be. So, choose to become a lion that you are!

CHAPTER SIXTEEN

UNMOVED BY CRITICISMS

Welcome, my boss, to another important area of this book; unmoved by criticism. How do you see criticism from people? Are you moved or troubled by what people say about you? Then I am here at the right time to tell you not to be moved by criticisms. Failure to create plans and to put them into action, because of what other people will think, do, or say. This enemy belongs at the head of the list, because it generally exists in one's unconscious mind, where its presence is not recognized.

Let us survey some of the indicators of the Fear of Criticism. The majority of people permit relatives, friends, and the public at large to so influence them that they cannot live their own lives, because they fear criticism. Vast numbers of people make mistakes in marriage, stand by the bargain, and go through life miserable and unhappy, because they fear criticism which may follow if they correct the mistake. Anyone who has submitted to this form of fear knows the irreversible damage it does, by destroying ambition, self- reliance, and the desire to achieve. Millions of people neglect to acquire belated educations, after having left school, because they fear criticism.

Countless numbers of men and women, both young and old, permit relatives to wreck their lives in the name of duty, because they fear criticism. Don't pay attention to critics. Ignore them my dear. Just acknowledge them as non-existence. You are the captain of your fate, the master of your soul. Duty does not require any person to submit to the destruction of his personal ambitions and the right to live his own life in his own way. People refuse to take chances in business, because they fear the criticism which may follow if they fail. The fear of criticism, in such cases, is stronger than the desire for success. Too many people refuse to set high goals for themselves, or even neglect selecting a career, because they fear the criticism of relatives and "friends" who may say, "Don't aim so high, people will think you are crazy."

Many people believe that material success is the result of favorable "breaks." There is an element of ground for the belief, but those depending entirely upon luck, are nearly always disappointed, because they overlook another important factor which must be present before one can be sure of success. It is the knowledge with which favorable "breaks" can be made to order. If one has persistence, one can get along very well without many other qualities. The only "break" anyone can afford to rely upon is a self-made "break." These come through the application of persistence. The preliminary point is definiteness of purpose.

Examine the first hundred people you meet, ask them what they want most in life, and ninety-eight of them will not be able to tell you. If you press them for an answer, some will say security, many will say money, a few will say happiness, others will say fame and power, and still others will say social recognition, ease in living, ability to sing, dance, or write, but none of them will be able to define these terms, or give the slightest indication of a strategy by which they hope to attain these vaguely expressed wishes. Riches do not respond to wishes. They respond only to definite plans, backed by definite desires, through constant persistence. How then can you develop persistence? Let us look at four simple steps into contact which lead to the habit of persistence. They call for no great amount of intelligence, no particular amount of education, and but little time or effort. The necessary steps are:

> A definite purpose backed by burning desire for its fulfillment.

> A definite plan, expressed in continuous action.

> A mind closed tightly against all negative and discouraging influences, including negative suggestions of relatives, friends and acquaintances.

> A friendly alliance with one or more persons who will encourage one to follow through with both plan and purpose.

These four steps are essential for success in all walks of life. The entire purpose of the principles of this philosophy is to enable one to take these four steps as a matter of habit. These are the steps by which one may control one's economic destiny. They are the steps that lead to freedom and independence of thought. They are the steps that lead to riches, in small or great quantities. They lead the way to power, fame, and worldly recognition. They are the four steps which guarantee favorable "breaks." They are the steps that convert dreams into physical realities. They lead, also, to the mastery of fear, discouragement, and indifference. Until you sacrifice the fear of people's opinions and what they think of you, you will remain beaten and broken till the day of your exit.

There is a magnificent reward for all who learn to take these four steps. It is the privilege of writing one's own ticket, and of making life yield whatever price is asked. What mystical power gives to men of persistence the capacity to master difficulties? Does the quality of persistence set up in one's mind some form of spiritual, mental or chemical activity which gives one access to supernatural forces? Does Infinite Intelligence throw itself on the side of the person who still fights on, after the battle has been lost, with the whole world on the opposing side? As one makes an impartial study of the prophets, philosophers, "miracle" men, and religious leaders of the past, one is drawn to the inevitable conclusion that persistence, concentration of effort, and definiteness of purpose, were the major sources of their achievements.

Just how man originally came by this fear, no one can state definitely, but one thing is certain; he has it in a highly developed form. The fear of criticism takes on many forms, the majority of which are petty and trivial. Why does the average person, even in this day of enlightenment, shy away from denying his belief in the fables which were the basis of most of the religions a few decades ago? The answer is, "Because of the fear of criticism." The fear of criticism robs man of his initiative, destroys his power of imagination, limits his individuality, takes away his self-reliance, and does him damage in a hundred other ways. Parents often do their children irreparable injury by criticizing them.

Samuel N. Adjovu, in his book; *"Dare to Differ; the Niche in the Labyrinths of Life"*, said "sometimes you need to be mocked, so that you can dig out the best in you. You need intimidators to kick your spirit of courage in. Sometimes you need people who will say 'NO' to bring you to a state of independence. I mean so that you don't get too comfortable with people's help. Disappointment is necessary sometimes to teach us how to cling to God alone. If the going gets tough, make your mind to either win or die".

Criticism is the one form of service, of which everyone has too much. Everyone has a stock of it which is handed out, gratis, whether called for or not. Employers who understand human nature, get the best there is in men, not by criticism, but by constructive suggestion. Parents may accomplish the same results with their children. Criticism will plant fear in the human heart, or resentment, but it will not build love or affection. I once read this statement from a friend of mine's WhatsApp status; *"Those who concluded about your shame shall end up in everlasting confusion plus disgrace"*. My boss, please don't allow criticisms to shut you down. Now is the time to override them and move on swiftly.

You might be feeling sad and wanting to quit trying. Yes, life is hard and sometimes you just can't comprehend why things happen the way they do. Just remember that God has the master key to every door of your life ang he will certainly do what He said He will do in your life. Be patient, keep trusting Him, keep loving those who hurt you, thinking you have no feelings too. The journey ahead is most important than accepting how people think of you and how they make you feel today. You don't allow them to distract you. The sun always shines when it is time to, so shall you shine when it is your time. Nothing is too late.it is only a matter of TIME if you keep the right attitude while waiting.

CHAPTER SEVENTEEN

WATCH YOUR TONGUE

King Solomon said in the book of Proverbs that '*life and death lies in the power of the tongue; and they that love it shall eat the fruit thereof*'. This simply means that whatever you say with your mouth and tongue come to pass. If you continue to proclaim negative things upon your life; only negative things will follow you. In the same way if you always declare positive things into your life; only positive and good things will follow. You therefore have the choice to say whatever you want to say but remember that the consequences are inevitable. What do you want to become in life? Start to declare them into your life.

Do you want to become a banker, doctor, engineer, teacher, nurse, teacher, police, etc. always declare, 'I shall become...' and never stop. Because your point of stopping is the end of your life. Govern your tongue, so that it will say nothing that will injure anyone around you. Practically all the injury that is done to a character, to a business, a home, or a person, is done with words. It is tongue work. The man or woman who makes no contribution to destructive thought and talk is a valuable asset anywhere. He is deaf to anything that is destructive to another. He is blind to anything that folks around him do. He cannot speak of it. He has mastery of himself. The efficiency of an office force is reduced sometimes by idle, unkind words. The man who can govern his temper, his tongue and his appetite, though he has but mediocre ability, is bound to get to the top.

When you say, "I will get that lesson," "I will conquer that subject," "I will master that problem," is your word worth anything? Do you make your word come true when you say, "I will give that up; I will put that thing over?" What is that word worth to you? Have faith in your own word? I am not asking what your word is worth outside. Pride may make you keep your word with people, but do you keep your word with yourself? You are too valuable to barter away the finest part of manhood or womanhood; your word. You are worth more to yourself, likely, than to anyone else, but by a year from now can you make yourself so valuable that men will pay any price for you? Great corporations are looking for men and women who can earn much annually.

Careless speaking is a vicious habit. When one realizes that his words are the coin of his kingdom, and that his words can be a cursing influence, or a blessing, he will learn to value the gift of speech. Control your tongue, or it will control you. You will often hear men say, "I speak my mind." "I have the freedom of speech". That is well if you have a good mind, but if your mind is poisoned, it is not good. An idle word spoken may fall into the soil of some one's heart and poison his whole life. What a blessing good conversation is and what a curse its opposite. Make your tongue a blessing, never a curse. A person is judged by his speech. Your words make you a blessing or a curse. Your words may carry a fortune in them. Learn to be master of your conversation.

I sometimes hear people say these words; It is no use. I might as well give it up. Every time I try, I only fail. Every job I get, I lose. Every money I get ahead; something happens and I have to use it. I am no farther ahead now that I was some years ago. There is something dead wrong somewhere. Hear me my boss, what has been the difficulty? You have the wrong slant on life. You have talked about your failing, your difficulties until they have become a mental disease. The most important thing to remember is that no matter what difficulties you have, no matter what problems you feel are holding you back, someone else, and probably thousands of other people, have had far greater obstacles to overcome than you could possibly dream of, and they have gone on to become successful nonetheless. And what others have done, you can do as well.

I venture to say that the last man of whom you sought to find employment read you like a book and said, "I don't want that man in my crew. He is a chronic fault finder." You have had so much trouble that you have eaten it, slept with it, dreamed it, until it oozes out of you. You may ask, "but how can I overcome it?" It is the easiest thing in the world to overcome. Solomon's solution was to, *"Trust in the Lord with all your heart and lean not upon thine own understanding. In all thy ways acknowledge the Lord and He will direct your path."* In other words, go into partnership with God where you cannot fail. There is no religion about this. You are dead wrong. Religion is a man-made thing. This is a God-made thing. This is common sense to link up with God. You take Jesus Christ as your Savior and you confess Him as your Lord. The moment you do this, you receive God's life and ability, and you cannot fail again. If you will walk with Him you can no more fail than Jesus failed. But Jesus failed on the cross, didn't He? Yes, but it was the greatest victory which came out of that failure that has ever been known. That was divine strategy. He will make you a conqueror if you walk with Him.

Let me share with you a story of a man who made it big in life by his words. This man started out in life without promoters, without a college education, without money. Someone said to him, "What have you beside your two hands to make a success of life?" He said softly, "I have nothing but words." The friend smiled, not understanding him. So, he started on his lonely quest for success with nothing but words. He learned the secret of putting things into words, of making words living things. He freighted his words with thought, clear thought, and, after a bit, he learned the secret of putting his fine, clean, splendid manliness into his words. Men began to set a value upon his words. People would stop him on the street to engage him in conversation just to hear his words. You understand that almost every man who has climbed to the top of the ladder of success has climbed with words. Here and there a man has climbed because of an unusual voice or an unusual gift of artistry, but the majority of men have gotten their feet on the first rung of the ladder of success by words. They climbed rung by rung to the top. A man must put a valuation on his own words before others will sense their value. The ambitious man's words became his bank account. He studied, he dug deep, he thought through on problems. Other people learned to trust his judgment and his words, rather than to study for themselves.

There is a vast army of people who have certain business ability, but they have to hire others to do most of their thinking. He supplied that want. He did the thinking. By and by they were willing to pay him almost any price to have him think for them. His words became valuable. They were his servants. How they laboured for him! He filled words with inspiration, with comfort, with hope for others. He sent them out on wings, until they passed from house to house, from lip to lip. He found himself being quoted here and there. His words were doing things. They were his servants working for him. He had learned the secret of words. By and by, publishers paid him almost unthinkable prices for his words. Why? Because he had learned the art of filling words with inspiration, new life. Let's study words. Let's learn to fill them with goodies for the children, healing for the sick, victory for the discouraged and we will win.

My dear brother and sister, words are very powerful. Words will put money into your pocket. Words will put proper food unto your table. Words will bless you and people around you. How can you talk anyhow after this topic? Mind your tongue. Control the words that emanate from your mouth. Just as you become what you think about, *you also become what you say to yourself.* The most powerful words you can repeat to yourself, especially if you are feeling tense or uneasy about an upcoming event, are the words, "I like myself! I like myself! I like myself!" Whenever you say, "I like myself!" your fears lessen and your courage increases. The words, "I like myself!" are so powerful and positive that they are immediately accepted by your subconscious mind as a command. They instantly affect your thoughts, feelings, and attitudes. Your body language immediately improves, and you stand straighter. Your face becomes more positive and cheerful. Your tone of voice becomes stronger and more confident. You feel better about yourself, and as a result, you treat everyone around you in a warmer, friendlier way.

Perhaps they never told you, but they grade you by your words. You are rated by your words. Your salary is gauged by the value of your words. Your words make a place for you in the business in which you are engaged. Neither jealousy nor fear can keep you from climbing to the top if your words have value that fits at the top. The organization is bound to give you the place that fits you if your words bring forth the right outcomes. You don't have to lay on; you don't have to amplify. All you have to do is to be natural, but make that "natural" worth listening to. Study your work. Study how to say things. Study how to use words that will change circumstances around you. Make a study, an analytical study of words, then see how much you can put into a single sentence. I don't mean how many words, but how much you can put into the words so that when men and women listen to your words, they will be thrilled by them. Here is a conversation that transpired in a bank. 'The bank security man said, "Good morning," in such a way that I turned to look at him. He had put something into his words. He had placed himself, his character into his words. His words rang. He directed me to the right teller. After I had left the bank. I felt inclined to go back and watch him deal with other customers.' Wow! What a warm reception it was. Cut out the useless words that stand in the way. Remove all the words that would hinder the thing you want to put over from reaching the mark. Make your words work in the hearts of those who listen.

Trust in words. Trust in the words of your own lips. Fill them with loving truth. Think in your heart of how you want to help those who are to be your customers or clients, how you are going to bless them and how the thing that you have is necessary to their satisfaction. It is what you put into your words that makes them live in the hearts of the hearers. Empty words die in no man's land. They never get over the trench. If they do, they are fiascos. If they do get across and people hear them, they amount to nothing. Living words; words bursting with heart messages; thrill and grip. Love always seeks the right word to convey its message without loss in transit. Clothe your thoughts in the most beautiful words, but don't sacrifice pungency for beauty. Blend them.

"Don't Break Me with Words"! This was Job's cry to his friends. remember Job was a servant of God who had gone through a lot of life catastrophe. His friends came as comforters but stayed as tormentors. Words heal and words break; words destroy and words make life as we find it today. Words heal us and words make us ill. Words bless us and words curse us. The words I just heard will dawdle through the day. How little women realize that a piercing, harsh, word in the morning will rob her husband of efficiency through a whole day. A loving, tender, beautiful word, a little prayer word will fill him with music that will lead him on to victory. We need the martial music of faith that only our loved ones can give to us. How little we have appreciated the tremendous power of words; written words, spoken words, words set to music.

A political aspirant said, "You won the election because you had better speakers than we. We had more money but we did not have words well spoken." You see, men and women, that study in words are one of the most valuable assets in a life. Learn how to make words work for you. Learn to make words burn. Learn to fill words with power that cannot be resisted. Mussolini held Italy in his hand by the power of his words. Austria was conquered by Hitler with words; no powder, no poison gas, no bayonets; just words. How we wait for a message made up of words. The secret of advancement in life lies in the ability to say the right kind of words. Mothers, your home atmosphere is a product of words. Your boy failed because wrong words were spoken, right words were not spoken. Why is it that some families grow up so clean and strong, fight their way through university and go out in life's fight and win? It is because the right kind of words were spoken in the home.

I remembered those days in the Senior High School. My uncle will always tell me "Vincent, I know you can make it…you must go straight to the University after Senior High…don't think of the Training College…I don't want you to go through the long way as me…" These words of my uncle always rung in my mind and continually pushed me through the Senior High and guess the final outcome. I finally went straight to the University. How powerful and wealthy your tongue can be if only you use it positively. Words make a child love education. Words bring a child to church or keep them away. Think of something of infinite importance and then learn to choose the right words to express it. Then send the words out with pen or tongue. The way we say it has fabulous weight.

Every public speaker should make a study of words, the kind of words that count. Then before he leaves his study, he should so charge his mind with God and God's ability that when he stands before the people that ability will fill his words until his people are electrified. He should make the delivery of words a training, an art. He should fill all his words with kindness, with love. Every man in the sales game should make himself a master of words. Try out words in your own home. See how they work. Fill your lips with lovely words, beautiful words, until men will love to meet you, long to hear you speak. Remember, words are apples of gold in network of silver.

Sometimes people fear to voice out what is inside them. Fear clips their powerful words. It is therefore very imperative for you to conquer your fears if you really want to make a difference and become successful. Stay focused as you read the next chapter.

CHAPTER EIGHTEEN

CONQUER YOUR FEARS

The primary difference between a rich person and a poor person is how they manages fear. Failure inspires winners. And failure defeats losers. It is the biggest secret of winners. It's the secret that losers do not know. The greatest secret of winners is that failure inspires winning; thus, they're not afraid of losing.

The fear of failure is the beginning of real failure. Dare to take that bold step and make that decision a reality. If you can't make up your mind decisively, then you'll never learn to make money anyway. Opportunities come and go. Being able to know when to make quick decisions is an important skill. The majority of people who fail to accumulate money sufficient for their needs, are, generally, easily influenced by the opinions of others. They permit the media and the gossiping neighbours to do their thinking for them. Opinions are the cheapest commodities on earth. Everyone has a flock of opinions ready to be wished upon anyone who will accept them.

If you are influenced by opinions when you reach decisions, you will not succeed in any undertaking, much less in that of transmuting your own desire into money. If you are influenced by the opinions of others, you will have no desire of your own. Keep your own counsel. Take no one into your confidence, except the members of your "Master Mind" group, and be very sure in your selection of this group, that you choose only those who will be in complete sympathy and harmony with your purpose. You are designed to conquer your challenges and prevail. It is your heritage to dominate the circumstances of your life. Nothing should stop you; if you've never planned to stop.

Fear of poverty is just a state of mind! But it is adequate to destroy one's chances of achievement in any undertaking, a truth which became painfully evident during any downturn. This fear paralyzes the faculty of reason, destroys the faculty of imagination, kills off self-reliance, demoralizes enthusiasm, discourages initiative, leads to uncertainty of purpose, encourages procrastination, wipes out enthusiasm, and makes self-control a no-no. It takes the charm from one's personality, destroys the possibility of accurate thinking, diverts concentration of effort, it impedes persistence, turns the will-power into nothingness, destroys ambition, beclouds the memory and invites failure in every conceivable form; it kills love and assassinates the finer emotions of the heart, discourages friendship and invites disaster in a hundred forms, leads to sleeplessness, misery and unhappiness and all this despite the obvious truth that we live in a world of over-abundance of everything the heart could desire, with nothing standing between us and our desires, excepting lack of a definite purpose.

Of all the ages of the world, of which we know anything, the age in which we live seems to be one that is outstanding because of man's money-madness. A man is considered less than the dust of the earth, unless he can display a fat bank account; but if he has money; never mind how he acquired it, he is a "king" or a "big shot"; he is above the law, he rules in politics, he dominates in business, and the whole world around him bows in respect when he passes. Nothing brings man so much suffering and humility as poverty! Only those who have experienced poverty understand the full meaning of this. It is no wonder that man fears poverty. Through a long line of inherited experiences man has learned that some men cannot be trusted where matters of money and earthly possessions are concerned. This is a rather stinging indictment, the worst part of it being that it is true.

The majority of marriages are motivated by the wealth possessed by one or both of the contracting partners. Many couples sign the contract of marriage not because they unconditionally love their partners but rather the material possession of the other partner. It is no wonder, therefore, that the divorce courts are always busy with divorce cases. So eager is man to possess wealth that he will acquire it in whatever manner he can; through legal methods if possible; through other dubious methods if necessary or expedient. You are very much like a great masterpiece enclosed in marble. But the marble that envelops you, and most other people, is the marble of small, limited thinking and excessive worry about the possibilities of loss or failure, rather than an excited anticipation of the rewards of success and achievement.

Thousands of men and women carry inferiority complexes with them all through life, because some well-meaning, but ignorant person destroyed their confidence through "opinions" or mockery. You have a brain and mind of your own- **use it!** and reach your own decisions. If you need facts or information from other people to enable you to reach decisions, as you probably will in many instances; acquire these facts or secure the information you need quietly, without disclosing your purpose. It is characteristic of people who have but a smattering or a veneer of knowledge to try to give the impression that they have much knowledge. Such people generally do too much talking, and too little listening. keep your eyes and ears wide open and your mouth closed, if you wish to acquire the habit of prompt decision. Those who talk too much do little. If you talk more than you listen, you do not only deprive yourself of many opportunities to accumulate useful knowledge, but you also disclose your plans and purposes to people who will take great delight in defeating you because they envy you.

Remember, also, that every time you open your mouth in the presence of a person who has an abundance of knowledge, you display to that person your exact stock of knowledge, or your lack of it! Genuine wisdom is usually conspicuous through modesty and silence. Keep in mind the fact that every person with whom you associate is, like yourself, seeking the opportunity to accumulate money. If you talk about your plans too freely, you may be surprised when you learn that some other person has beaten you to your goal by putting into action ahead of you the plans of which you talked unwisely. Let one of your first decisions be to keep a closed mouth and open ears and eyes. What had I been saying all this while? What I am saying is that gather courage, eliminate fear, and decide to take action now.

Take the risk of program you dreaming about. marry early? it. Is it about

> *"Hard times never last, but tough people do."*
>
> Samuel. N. Adjovu

pursuing that have been Do you want to Be bold about initiating a developmental project? Do it now! Don't procrastinate! Dreams are like the invisible angels that pulls us up high to the sky, helping us fly beyond limitations, to see and explore the world in a different way, realizing the beauty of it all. Go get that dream! Even when it hurts, keep moving and keep this at the back of your mind: hard times never last, but tough people do. Never go back; always forward to the grand finale of success. Nothing great comes without hard work so stay strong and keep going. With all that said, it is indeed not as easy to be said than done.

Conquering your fear especially when you're not used to it or even having the courage to fight against it often cause us to back out from our initial plans and goals. The darkness always tries to corrupts and over-shined your tiny little light in you. But always remember, "Light always wins over darkness" You are stronger than you think you are! If you want something, go get it!

Sometimes the things that scare us are the things that grasp our great treasure.

Regardless of how hard it is, and how many times you have failed, try harder! Make every failure an achievement to stop you from making the same old mistakes again. All successful people start from the basics. A strong foundation can lead to a better construction of a concrete building. Regardless of what circumstances or opportunity you have, please do not fly without learning how to fly. A good story always comes from the heart. Be an "Explorer" to discover an endless journey that lies ahead. Never let your fire diminish without even trying. with great effort comes great results! If it fails, try harder!! may you be the best part of you, never let anyone judge you because they aren't you! Decide that you will do this, no matter what.

You know I will always like to make any point in this book with reference to the holy manual through which you and I were created. The scripture says *"for God has not given us the spirit of fear, but of power, love, and of a sound mind."* Did you hear that? If you don't have fear in your manual then why are you afraid? Don't be afraid of the world that takes away and suck everything from you. Why are you afraid to take up that challenge in which lies an opportunity for success? I mean tell me what your fear is and I will tell you to revisit your manual- God. There are so many scriptures I can vividly say spoke against fear.

But I won't bore you now with them. I will reserve them for another time.

Have you ever come across the Chinese internet guru- Jack Ma? Listen to what he said when he was interviewed by one of the American hosts of youth empowerment. *"Fail big! Don't be afraid to take a chance. Don't be afraid to go outside the box. Don't be afraid to fail big, and to dream big."* Reason makes the plans. The strong one carries them through. The strong one is your Will. Dream, then carry out your dreams. Drive yourself to the finish line. The Will-less dreamer is never a success. You have the vision. Make it come to pass. You dream your dream, and then make the dream come true. Cultivate a discontent with everything that is common in yourself. Compel yourself to improve your mind, your natural abilities. If you have the gift of cooking, be the best cook in the community. If you have a gift, no matter what it is, make that gift stand out until men will admire it. Then someone will want to pay the price for it.

There are few who have reached the top who have not been handicapped. Obstacles stand in the way of the man who climbs. I don't know why this is, but I know it is true. These obstacles have to be overcome, but in the overcoming process, one fits himself for places of responsibility. I appreciate the existence of poverty, need of self-denial, self-culture, long hours of study and hard work. The inward drive to plod on when tired is the thing which makes men strong, self-reliant conquerors. Every failure stimulates them to harder work. There is no giving up. There is no yielding. Facing impossible circumstances becomes a daily experience to the conqueror. He learns to win. He has cultivated the will to win, the will to conquer. He kept the fires of ambition burning. He has made work a part of himself. He is a master. He is the man who uses the public library and secondhand book stores. He is ever studying to improve himself in his place. He knows his trade, his business, his profession. He makes himself an authority in his particular field. He counts his handicaps a blessing. He goes on with God and wins. No man is a failure until he lies down and the undertaker puts him under the grass.

Learn how to overcome your fears. Life always present us hard lessons that must be accommodated. If you learn these lessons, you will grow into a wise, wealthy, and happy person. If you don't, you will spend your life blaming a job, low pay, or your boss for your problems. You'll live life always hoping for that big break that will solve all your money problems. If you're the kind of person who has no guts, you just give up every time life pushes you. If you're that kind of person, you'll live all your life playing it safe, doing the right things, saving yourself for some event that never happens. Then you die a boring old man. You'll have lots of friends who really like you because you were such a nice hardworking guy. But the truth is that you let life push you into submission. Deep down you were terrified of taking risks. You really wanted to win, but the fear of losing was greater than the excitement of winning. Deep inside, you and only you will know you didn't go for it.

You chose to play it safe. Just know that it's fear that keeps most people working at a job: the fear of not paying their bills, the fear of being fired, the fear of not having enough money, and the fear of starting over. That's the price of studying to learn a profession or trade, and then working for money. Most people become a slave to money and then get angry at their boss.

Fear is the unhealthy child of anxiety and nonbelief. Those two are married and what children they have begotten! Fear leads to the wasting of vital energy, the disturbing of digestive and other organs, which impairs your ability. It becomes a mental disease. Almost everyone has it. It is spreadable. It leads to all kinds of physical and mental disorders. It's cure is simple: "*Trust in the Lord with all thy heart, and lean not upon thine own understanding. In all thy ways give Him His place and He will direct thy paths.*" Or, "*Casting all your anxiety upon Him for He careth for you.*" Get quiet for a moment and remember this: God is on your side. If God is for you, who can be against you? They can't conquer the man who trusts in the Lord with all his heart.
There aren't enough enemies in all the world to whip the man who trusts absolutely in the wisdom of God his Father and does not lean upon his own knowledge.

No man is safe to go out into the business world, until he has first learned the secret of absolute trust in the Lord. So, if you haven't learned it yet and you are bearing your burdens with fretting and care and anxiety, go alone and settle the great issue with Him. Take His wisdom and grace to go out and do your work with perfect efficiency. Don't forget the title of the book you are reading now. *Arise and Make a Difference; the Drive Behind Success.* Your ability to overcome all your fear is the beginning of making a difference in life.

The journey into this book is far but you proved beyond all reasonable doubt that you are ready to make a difference. Just take a look at an interesting story in the next chapter.

CHAPTER NINETEEN

THE STAR FISH STORY

"Don't be like everyone else because no one can be like you"

A story has been narrated about star fish to metaphorically portray a lesson about making a difference in life. Read it carefully and make your decision out of it. There had been a storm the day before. The beach was littered with debris left by the pounding waves. There was a driftwood, rope, seaweed and all sort of things. Overwhelmingly, there were starfish. Thousands of them. It was a warm morning and the starfish were stranded. They would certainly die as the sun got hotter. Some were obviously dry and brittle and beyond help. But others were still alive. Walking along the beach were a young lady and her mother. They strolled along, making the most of the blue sky and the sunshine. They were just enjoying the day and each other's company. As they walked, the older woman would often bend down and pick up a starfish, and throw it back into the water.

The younger woman watched what her mother was doing, and finally she said, "why on earth are you throwing these starfish back into the water?" The older woman replied, "the starfish fish will die in this sun if they are left on the beach." The younger woman said, "millions of starfish on thousands of beaches all over the world are dying everyday so why bother? You aren't making any difference. What you are doing is so futile. One starfish at a time is not changing anything." Her mother just smiled in a kind way. She walked over to another starfish. She bent down, and picked it up and threw it back into the water… it made a difference… to that one," she said. Hear me. It's not that we are blind to the problems, or self-centered and just don't care. Mostly it's because we are so overwhelmed by how huge the problems are and just how much suffering there is. We ask ourselves how can we help? I am just one person and there are just so much need. What can just one person do on their own? I hope you are not one of such people? The ball is right in your court to make a choice now.

If you can person smile, loved and kindness and have made a the biggest can make in life is to make another laugh, or feel treat them with respect then you difference. One of differences you someone else's encourage them.

> *"Every time you smile at someone, it is an action of love, a gift to a person, a beautiful thing"*
> **Mother Teresa**

But how can you encourage someone when you are sinking sand yourself? Boss! Yes! I called you boss again because I know deep inside you lies a potent seed of putting smile on someone else face. Rise up my good friend and put yourself together. First of all, encourage yourself. Tell yourself you can do it! Remind yourself of your kingship. Kings don't beg for food. No! kings don't live their life anyhow. Kings influence and impact their subjects and followers because they are great leaders. Make life easy for others. No! I don't want to hear you remind me of your past. I know your past. I know you went through hell to get to where you are now. In fact, I know you are still going through some tough times now. But even in the midst of all these catastrophes lies your greatness.

Please don't let this great opportunity pass by you. Now is the time to shine. Now is the time to make the difference. Grab that opportunity now. I believe in you. Dale Carnegie said, "abilities wither under criticisms; they blossom under encouragement." Today I encourage you to rise up and pick up your cross of victory and walk towards success. Go and make an overwhelmingly great difference in the world. Begin now! Please don't put it off a moment longer. You already have all it takes to make the world a better place. Making a difference may seem like a huge task, but all it takes is the willingness of just ONE person. Together we all can make a difference. One person, one small act or one starfish at a time. Keep helping others because you will one day become successful.

Life goes on. Years unfold, months goes, weeks goes, and days also unfold with time. You've got to understand that to achieve these goals you must apply discipline and consistency. You have to work at it. Every day you have to plan towards it. Working really hard is what successful people do. Remember that just because you are doing a lot does not mean you are getting a lot done. Yes! There is more to add up. Bill Gate is not satisfied with his current level of worth. Neither is Jack Ma of Alibaba nor Mark Zuckerberg of Facebook satisfied of their status. Don't confuse movement with progress. The fact that you notice some movement from your current level does not necessarily mean you are actually progressing in life. No! that could be very deceptive. Go higher. Listen! It is not how much you have but what you do with what you have. *"Don't just aspire to make a living. Aspire to make a difference"* (Denzel Wasshington)

CHAPTER TWENTY

THE RICH AND THE POOR

There is gold everywhere. Most people are not trained to see it.

You are welcome to a very exciting topic of this book you are reading now. Let me open you up with this personal quote of mine; *"The difference between the rich and the poor is <u>sacrifice</u>."* If you really want to become rich someday then learn how to sacrifice. Be ready to give up the things you find pleasure in doing. Learn to give up excessive time on social media, games, unnecessary argument, and many more you personally know takes much of your time. Be the first person who will ever ask great and successful people to teach you how to make money. Don't be eager to be an employee. Employees ask for a job and a paycheck, but never to be taught about money. So, most will spend the best years of their lives working for money, not really understanding what it is they are working for.

The rich don't work for money. Only the poor work for money. When you work for money then payment of taxes is inevitable. When your dream of working is to get money then I can confidently tell you that the probability of losing that job is very high. Don't be an educated poor person. If your vision of going to school is to obtain a paper certificate, then you are doomed for life. Don't go to school to end up seeking for job. Please change that mindset now! Come out of school and create your own work. Listen! I didn't say don't work for anyone after school. Of course, you need to work for others to establish yourself financially then you can start your own work. But don't let that work be your life long job. Go to school. Get all the degrees that you can. But don't let your grades judge your abilities because you are as good as God sees you. Most people want everyone else in the world to change but themselves. Let me tell you, it's easier to change yourself than everyone else.

The rich learn the subject of financial education. The poor only go to school to learn how to work for others. Most people go to college for four years, and their education ends. Most people never study the subject 'money'. They go to work, get their paycheck, balance their checkbooks, and that's it. Then they wonder why they have money problems. They think that more money will solve the problem and don't realize that it's their lack of financial education that is the problem. Most people want to go to school, learn a profession, have fun at their work, and earn lots of money. One day they wake up with big money problems, and then they can't stop working. That's the price of only knowing how to work for money instead of studying how to have money work for you. So, do you still have the passion to learn?

Life doesn't teach you an easy method of becoming successful and making a difference. Life is the best teacher of all. Most of the time, life does not talk to you. It just sorts of pushes you around. Each push is life saying, 'Wake up. There's something I want you to learn.' If you learn life's lessons, you will do well. If not, life will just continue to push you around. People do two things. Some just let life push them around. Others get angry and push back. But they push back against their boss, or their job, or their husband or wife. They do not know its life that's pushing. Life pushes all of us around. Some people give up and others fight. A few learn the lesson and move on. They welcome life pushing them around. To these few people, it means they need and want to learn something. They learn and move on. Most people quit and a few like you fight.

I want you to get angry at your current level. Never be satisfied at any level you find yourself. There is more up there waiting for your capture. I'm glad you are getting angry now about working for someone. I repeat, be prepared to learn. You see, true learning takes energy, passion, and a burning desire. Anger is a big part of that formula, for passion is anger and love combined. When it comes to money, most people want to play it safe and feel secure. So, passion does not direct them. Fear does. The main cause of poverty or financial struggle is fear and ignorance, not the economy or the government or the rich. It's self-inflicted fear and ignorance that keep people trapped. What intensifies fear and desire is ignorance. That is why rich people with lots of money often have more fear the richer they get. I just want to reiterate that never forget that fear and desire can lead you into life's biggest trap if you're not aware of them controlling your thinking.

Arise and Make a Difference; the Drive Behind Success

To spend your life living in fear, never exploring your dreams, is cruel. To work hard for money, thinking that it will buy you things that will make you happy is also painful. To wake up in the middle of the night terrified about paying bills is an awful way to live. To live a life dictated by the size of a paycheck is not really living a life. Thinking that a job makes you secure is lying to yourself. That's painful, and that's the snare I want you to avoid. I've seen how money runs people's lives. Don't let that happen to you. Please don't let money run your life.

Most people have a price. And they have a price because of human emotions named fear and greed. Foremost, the fear of being without money motivates us to work hard, and then once we get that paycheck, greed or desire starts us thinking about all the wonderful things money can buy. The pattern is then set. The pattern of get up, go to work, pay bills; get up, go to work, pay bills. People's lives are forever controlled by two emotions: fear and greed. Offer them more money and they continue the cycle by increasing their spending. The rich conquer their greedy desire for more money. It's perfectly normal to desire something better, prettier, more fun, or exciting. So, people also work for money because of desire. They desire money for the joy they think it can buy. But the joy that money brings is often short-lived, and they soon need more money for more joy, more pleasure, more comfort, and more security. So, they keep working, thinking money will soothe their souls that are troubled by fear and desire.

But money can't do that. I just want you to have a chance to avoid the trap caused by those two emotions, fear and desire. Use them in your favor, not against you.

CHAPTER TWENTY-ONE

FINANCIAL INTELLEGENCE

It's not how much money you make. It's how much money you keep. (Robert T. Kiyosaki)

Congratulations my boss for coming this far in this journey of *"Arise and Make a Difference; The Drive Behind Success."* You are welcome to another imperative topic of discussion as far as this book is concern. Financial intelligence is a very powerful key to making a difference in life. Your ability to amass financial knowledge is a step to becoming successful in life. Relax and enjoy the reading.

Most people fail to realize that in life, it's not how much money you make. It's how much money you keep. We've all heard stories of lottery winners who are poor, then suddenly rich, and then poor again. They win millions, yet are soon back where they started. Or stories of professional athletes and footballers who at the age of 20-25years are earning millions, but are struggling to survive after some few years later. I know so many people who became instant millionaires. And while I am glad some people have become richer and richer, my caution is that in the long run, it's not how much money you make. It's how much you keep, and how many generations you keep it.

Most people struggle financially because they do not know the difference between an asset and a liability. Rich people acquire assets. The poor and middle class acquire liabilities that they think are assets. An asset is something that puts money in your pocket. A liability is something that takes money out of your pocket. This is really all you need to know. If you want to be rich, simply spend your life buying assets. If you want to be poor or middle class, spend your life buying liabilities. If your pattern is to spend everything you get, most likely an increase in cash will just result in an increase in spending. Thus, the saying, "A fool and his money is one big party".

Maybe you are a student, I want to encourage you not to leave school without any financial skill. Don't be like other graduate who after school have their life shut in misery because of limited financial knowledge. Because students leave school without financial skills, millions of educated people pursue their profession successfully, but later find themselves struggling financially. They work harder but don't get ahead. What is missing from their education is not how to make money, but how to manage money. It's called financial aptitude what you do with the money once you make it, how to keep people from taking it from you, how to keep it longer, and how to make that money work hard for you. Most people don't understand why they struggle financially because they don't understand cash flow. A person can be highly educated, professionally successful, and financially illiterate. These people often work harder than they need to because they learned how to work hard, but not how to have their money work hard for them.

Many people ask others how to get more money rather how to keep money. They don't understand that their trouble is really how they choose to spend the money they do have. This is caused by financial illiteracy and not understanding the difference between an asset and a liability. More money seldom solves someone's money problems. Intelligence solves problems. If you find out that you have dug yourself into a hole... stop digging. All too often, the poor and middle class allow the power of money to control them. By simply getting up and working harder, failing to ask themselves if what they do makes sense, they shoot themselves in the foot as they leave for work every morning. By not fully understanding money, the vast majority of people allow its awesome power to control them.

When it comes to houses, most people work all their lives paying for a home they never own. In other words, most people buy a new house every few years, each time incurring a new 30-year loan to pay off the previous one. The greatest losses of all are those from missed opportunities. If all your money is tied up in your house, you may be forced to work harder because your money continues blowing out of the expense column, instead of adding to the asset column; the classic middle-class cash-flow pattern. If a young couple would put more money into their asset column early on, their later years would be easier. Their assets would have grown and would be available to help cover expenses. All too often, a house only serves as a vehicle for incurring a home-equity loan to pay for mounting expenses. Too often, people count their house and savings and retirement plans as all they have as their asset. Because they have no money to invest, they simply don't invest. This costs them investment experience. Most never become what the investment world calls "a sophisticated investor." And the best investments are usually first sold to sophisticated investors, who then turn around and sell them to the people playing it safe.

Most often I hear people say that the rich will always be rich and the poor will remain poor. This statement always triggers an important question in my mind that I always look for an opportunity to express it. I see this platform to be the best place to ask this question; why is the rich always rich and the poor is always poor?" well, you the answer to this question may be subjective to personal opinions. In my opinion, the rich get richer because they focus on getting more assets than liabilities. The assets of the rich generates more than enough income to cover expenses, with the balance reinvested into the asset column. The asset column continues to grow and, therefore, the income it produces grows with it. The result is that the rich get richer! The poor on the other hand focus on acquiring more liabilities such as cars, houses, etc. than possessing assets.

The middle class finds itself in a constant state of financial struggle. Their primary income is through their salary. as their wages increase, so do their taxes. their expenses tend to increase in proportion to their salary increase. They treat their home as their primary asset, instead of investing in income-producing assets. This pattern of treating your home as an investment, and the idea that a pay raise means you can buy a larger home or spend more, is the foundation of today's debt-ridden society. increased spending throws families into greater debt and into more financial uncertainty, even though they may be advancing in their jobs and receiving raises on a regular basis. This is high-risk living caused by weak financial education. The massive loss of jobs in recent times proves how shaky the middle class really is financially unschooled. Company pension plans are being replaced, social security is obviously in trouble and can't be relied upon as a source for retirement. panic has set in for the middle class. Today, mutual funds are popular because they supposedly represent safety. average mutual-fund buyers are too busy working to pay taxes and mortgages, save for their children's college, and pay off credit cards. they do not have time to study investing, so they rely on the expertise of the manager of a mutual fund. Also, because the mutual fund includes many different types of investments, they feel their money is safer because it is "diversified." This educated middle class subscribes to the doctrine put out by mutual-fund brokers and financial planners: "play it safe. avoid risk."

The real tragedy is that the lack of early financial education is what creates the risk faced by average middle-class people. the reason they have to play it safe is because their financial positions are tenuous at best. Their balance sheets are not balanced. Instead, they are loaded with liabilities and have no real assets that generate income. Typically, their only source of income is their paycheck. their livelihood becomes entirely dependent on their employer. So, when genuine deals of a lifetime come along, these people can't take advantage of them because they are working so hard, are taxed to the max, and are loaded with debt. Keep liabilities and expenses down so more money is available to continue pouring into the asset column. Soon the asset base will be so deep that you can afford to look at more speculative investments. Most people work for everyone but themselves. They work first for the owners of the company, then for the government through taxes, and finally for the bank that owns their mortgage.

Our current educational system focuses on preparing today's youth to get good jobs by developing scholastic skills. Their lives will revolve around their wages or, as described earlier, their income column. Many will study further to become engineers, scientists, cooks, police officers, artists, writers, and so on. These professional skills allow them to enter the workforce and work for money. A problem with school is that you often become what you study. So, if you study cooking, you become a chef. If you study the law, you become an attorney, and a study of auto mechanics makes you a mechanic. The mistake in becoming what you study is that too many people forget to mind their own business. They spend their lives minding someone else's business and making that person rich. So many people have put themselves in deep financial trouble when they run short of income. To raise cash, they sell their assets. But their personal assets can generally be sold for only a fraction of the value that is listed on their personal balance sheet. Or if there is a gain on the sale of the assets, they are taxed on the gain. So again, the government takes its share, thus reducing the amount available to help them out of debt.

My boss, keep expenses low, reduce liabilities, and diligently build a base of solid assets. For young people who have not yet left home, it is important for parents to teach them the difference between an asset and a liability. Get them to start building a solid asset column before they leave home, get married, buy a house, have kids, and get stuck in a risky financial position, clinging to a job, and buying everything on credit. I see so many young couples who get married and trap themselves into a lifestyle that will not let them get out of debt for most of their working years. For many people, just as the last child leaves home, the parents realize they have not adequately prepared for retirement and they begin to scramble to put some money away. Then their own parents become ill and they find themselves with new responsibilities.

Once we leave school, most of us know that it is not so much a matter of college degrees or good grades that count. In the real world outside of academics, something more than just grades are required. I have heard it called many things; guts, chutzpah, balls, audacity, bravado, cunning, daring, tenacity, and brilliance. This factor, whatever it is labeled, ultimately decides one's future much more than school grades do. Inside each of us is one of these brave, brilliant, and daring characters. In my personal understanding, your financial genius requires both technical knowledge as well as courage.

If fear is too strong, the genius is suppressed. In my interaction with people I strongly urge them to learn to take risks, to be bold, and to let their genius convert that fear into power and brilliance. It works for some and just terrifies others. I have come to realize that for most people, when it comes to the subject of money, they would rather play it safe. But then I will discourage you from playing it safe. There are huge changes up ahead. In the coming years, there will be more people just like the young inventor Alexander Graham Bell. There will be a hundred people like Bill Gates and hugely successful companies like Microsoft created every year, all over the world. And there also will be many more bankruptcies, layoffs, and downsizings.

I find so many people struggling today, often working harder, simply because they cling to old ideas. They want things to be the way they were, and they resist change. I know people who are losing their jobs or their houses, and they blame technology or the economy or their boss. Sadly, they fail to realize that they might be the problem. Old ideas are their biggest liability. It is a liability simply because they fail to realize that while that idea or way of doing something was an asset yesterday, yesterday is gone. I have seen people pull a great opportunity card, read it out loud, and have no idea that it is a great opportunity. They have the money, the time is right, they have the card, but they can't see the opportunity staring them in the face. They fail to see how it fits into their financial plan. Most people have an opportunity of a lifetime flash right in front of them, and they fail to see it. A year later, they find out about it, after everyone else got rich. The single most powerful asset we all have is our mind. If it is trained well, it can create enormous wealth seemingly instantaneously. An untrained mind can also create extreme poverty that can crush a family for generations.

Financial intelligence is basically having more options. If the opportunities aren't coming your way, what else can you do to improve your financial position? If an opportunity lands in your lap and you have no money and the bank won't talk to you, what else can you do to get the opportunity to work in your favor? If your hunch is wrong, and what you've been counting on doesn't happen, how can you turn a lemon into millions? That is financial intelligence. It is not so much what happens, but how many different financial solutions you can think of to turn a lemon into millions. It is how creative you are in solving financial problems. Most people only know one solution:

Work hard, save, and borrow. So why would you want to increase your financial intelligence? Because you want to be the kind of person who creates your own luck. You take whatever happens and make it better. Few people realize that luck is created, just as money is. And if you want to be luckier and create money instead of working hard, then your financial intelligence is important. If you are the kind of person who is waiting for the right thing to happen, you might wait for a long time. It's like waiting for all the traffic lights to be green for five miles before you'll start your trip.

The idea in anything is to use your technical knowledge, wisdom, and love of the game to cut the odds down, to lower the risk. Of course, there is always risk. It is financial intelligence that improves the odds. Thus, what is risky for one person is less risky to someone else. That is the primary reason I will constantly encourage you to invest more in financial education. The smarter you are, the better chance you have of beating the odds. Most people never get wealthy simply because they are not trained financially to recognize opportunities right in front of them. Most people never win because they're more afraid of losing. Going to school is very important. But the methods of delivery in school can be very meaningless. In school we learn that mistakes are bad, and we are punished for making them. Yet if you look at the way humans are designed to learn; we learn by making mistakes. We learn to walk by falling down. If we never fell down, we would never walk. The same is true for learning to ride a bike. I still have scars on my legs, but today I can ride a bike, even motor cycle without thinking. The same is true for getting rich. Unfortunately, the main reason most people are not rich is because they are terrified of losing. Winners are not afraid of losing. But losers are.

Failure is part of the process of success. People who avoid failure also avoid success. Great opportunities are not seen with your eyes. They are seen with your mind. If you want to be successful faster, you must double your rate of failure. Success lies on the far side of failure. The fact is that the more you have already failed, the more likely it is you are on the verge of great success. Your failures have prepared you to succeed. This is why a streak of good luck seems to follow a streak of bad luck. When in doubt, double your rate of failure. The more things you *try*, the more likely you are to *triumph*. You overcome your fears only by doing the thing you fear until the fear has no more control over you.

To find million-dollar "deals of a lifetime" requires us to call on our financial genius. I believe that each of us has a financial genius within us. The problem is that our financial genius lies asleep, waiting to be called upon. It lies asleep because our culture has educated us into believing that the

> **Rich people acquire assets. The poor and middle class acquire liabilities that they think are assets**

love of money is the root of all evil. It has encouraged us to learn a profession so we can work for money, but failed to teach us how to have money work for us. It taught us not to worry about our financial future because our company or the government would take care of us when our working days are over. However, it is our children, educated in the same school system, who will end up paying for this absence of financial education. The message is still to work hard, earn money, and spend it, and when we run short, we can always borrow more. If you ask most people if they would like to be rich or financially free, they would say yes. But then reality sets in. The road seems too long with too many hills to climb. It's easier to just work for money and hand the excess over to your broker.

One of the hardest things about wealth-building is to be true to yourself and to be willing to not go along with the crowd. This is because, in the market, it is usually the crowd that shows up late that is slaughtered. If a great deal is on the front page, it's too late in most instances. Look for a new deal. As we used to say as surfers: "There is always another wave." People who hurry and catch a wave late usually are the ones who wipe out. Smart investors don't time the markets. If they miss a wave, they search for the next one and get themselves in position. This is hard for most investors because buying what is not popular is frightening. Timid investors are like sheep going along with the crowd. Or their greed gets them in when wise investors have already taken their profits and moved on.

Wise investors buy an investment when it's not popular. They know their profits are made when they buy, not when they sell. They wait patiently. As I said, they do not time the market. Just like a surfer, they get in position for the next big swell. You will achieve financial success only after you accept that everything that you ever become is completely up to you. You are responsible. No one is going to do it for you. Keep repeating, *"If it's to be, it's up to me!"*

I hope you've been enjoying the lesson so far and you are poised to take action immediately. Great! That's exactly what I want to know.

CHAPTER TWENTY-TWO

MIND YOUR HABITS

Congratulations! I warmly welcome you to another area of this novel. Isn't it interesting to possess a knowledge of what habits are and how you can harness them into success? If it is, then enjoy the reading. A habit is a routine of behavior that is repeated regularly and tends to occur subconsciously. Habits are more or less fixed way of thinking, willing, or feeling acquired through previous repetition of a mental experience. Form habits of study, habits of business. Learn to save the moments; the hours will take care of themselves. Form the habit of concentration, downright hard thinking. Drive your mind. Become an absolute slave driver over your own faculties. They are your slaves, your servants. Make them work. Make them study. Make them develop. Destroy indolence and that buzzing habit of dreaming. Cultivate the habit of thorough work.

The great artists, writers, musicians, and poets became great because they acquired the habit of relying upon the "still small voice" which speaks from within through the faculty of creative imagination. It is a fact well known to people who have "keen" imaginations that their best ideas come through so-called "hunches." Analysis of people who had accrued fortunes well beyond the million-dollar mark, disclosed the fact that every one of them had the habit of reaching decisions promptly and of changing these decisions slowly, if and when they were changed. People who fail to accrue money, without exception, have the habit of reaching decisions if at all, very slowly, and of changing these decisions quickly and often. Create a habit that builds a strong body and a strong mind. Set your found action for a strong day which will lead to a better habit and in time into a better life.

Successful people are those who have developed the habits of success. Successful people form good habits and ensure that those habits govern their behaviors. He has a group of very fine habits. He has the habit of study, the habit of control of his eyes and ears, the control of his passions and ambitions. Unsuccessful people allow bad habits to form, and these bad habits then lead to frustration and failure. Successful people are simply those who developed successful habits. They have trained themselves, like athletes, to do certain things in a certain way, over and over again, until they do them automatically, without even thinking about them.

One of the habits of success is that of *early rising*. Successful people get up a little bit earlier, read and prepare, plan and organize their day on paper in advance, and get going before the average person has even started. Successful people make a habit of getting up early, usually by 6:00 or 6:30 in the morning, sometimes earlier, and then getting going immediately. This gives them a great jump on the day. The average person, on the other hand, takes a full hour to get up and get going in the morning. Then they drag themselves off to work, thinking about lunchtime, and what they are going to do in the evening. When *your* alarm clock goes off, get up immediately and get going right away. Start moving. Develop the habit of rising early and starting right to work on your most important task. This habit can do as much to assure your success as any other habit you develop.

Develop the habit of moving fast. Successful people in every field have a sense of urgency. Only a small percentage of the population moves quickly when opportunity or responsibility presents itself. You must be a member of this small percentage.

CHAPTER TWENTY-THREE

LET GO OF THE PAST

"Remember your present situation isn't your final destination; there expect more and let go the past."

Hello my boss, you are welcome to another crucial topic of this novel; *let go the past*. If you really want to arise and make a difference in your life then you've got to forget everything that occurred or happened to you in the past and focus on the present and future. The Apostle Paul, in his epistle to the Philippians, said, **"Brethren, I count not myself to have apprehended: but this one thing I do, forgetting those things which are behind, and reaching forth unto those things which are before, I press toward the mark for the prize of the high calling of God in Christ Jesus".** There are two time periods in life, the past and the future. The present is only a brief, fleeting moment. You can choose to focus your attention on what has happened, which cannot be changed, or on the future, on what is possible, over which you have some control.

Many people spend most of their emotional energies being upset and angry about events that occurred in the past. Unfortunately, this energy is completely wasted. Nothing good can come of constantly complaining about the past. Even worse, the negative emotions kept alive by reliving past events rob you of the joy and excitement that you could experience by thinking about future possibilities.

Arise and Make a Difference; the Drive Behind Success

It seemed that most unhappy people are held back by some event that occurred in the past that they cannot let go of. They are still resentful, angry, or depressed over something that someone did or did not do or say. They are mad at one or both parents, a sibling, a previous relationship or marriage, a boss or business relationship, a failed investment or financial mistake. You failed yesterday and so what? You were a teen mother or father and so what? Who told you, that you cannot have that dream? Let go the past and look forward to the future. The future is where your promises are. So, get up and gear up because your glorious future is unfolding. Lift your eyes and see the path of greatness ahead of you; it is the reason why you are still here in the world while others are gone. Position yourself for what the world had never seen and be ready to rule your wrecks.

The fact is that your life will be a nonstop series of problems, difficulties, setbacks, and temporary failures. These unpredicted and unwanted hitches and disappointments are a normal, natural, and inevitable fact of growing up. To change your thinking and change your life, you must make a decision to get over them and to get on with your life, no matter what happened. Until you do, you remain a slave to the past, which cannot be changed in any case.

Probably, someone might have overcome you in one area or field of work and you might have kept that hatred in you. I came to tell you to let go of it. The sooner you let go of it the better your chances of making a huge difference and become very successful in life. You can learn anything you need to learn, to accomplish any goal you can set for yourself. Generally speaking, no one is smarter than **YOU**, and no one is better than **YOU**. Just because someone is doing better than you doesn't mean that he *is* better than you. It usually means that he has just learned how to succeed in his particular field before you have. And whatever someone else has done, you can probably do as well

Most people are trapped by the psychological effect of *"Learned Helplessness"*, a situation where an individual think he/she can't do anything about a difficult situation he/she find themselves with. As the result of childhood experiences, especially destructive criticism and early failure experiences, people eventually reach the point where they feel helpless to change or to take action in different areas of their lives. The majority of men and women feel overwhelmed by things that seem to happen to them, and the many things going on around them. They feel that there is nothing they can do to influence events or to improve their lives. The most obvious proof that an individual is experiencing learned helplessness is the repeated use of the words **"I can't."**

People feel that they can't lose weight, can't get a better job, can't improve or change their relationships, can't increase their incomes, can't upgrade their knowledge and skills, and can't do many other things that they really want to do. They have tried unsuccessfully so many times in the past that they have come to conclude automatically that there is very little they can do to change the future. They become passive and accepting of their situations. Their lives consist of getting up in the morning, going to work, socializing a bit, coming home, eating dinner, watching television for four or five hours, and then going off to bed. It's time to let go of all those fears and rise up to greatness. No matter how many times you fall, you must rise again and keep going because you might die tomorrow and all will be over forever. If you fail an exam, quiz, or any assessment tool today, it doesn't mean that you cannot pass it again tomorrow. You are a spectacular creation bound on a voyage, make sure you sail through till the end.

Another mental condition that holds people back is called the *"comfort zone."* Human beings are creatures of habit. They begin an activity of any kind and they soon become comfortable with it. They then become extremely reluctant to change what they are doing, or change the situation they are in, even if they are not particularly happy or satisfied with it. They become somewhat content and complacent. Eventually, they become afraid to change, for any reason. They get into a rut, and the longer they stay in their rut, the deeper it grows, until they finally give up all hope of ever changing or improving their lives. *Learned helplessness,* in amalgamation with the *comfort zone,* creates a person who feels trapped and helpless, weak and powerless, and unable to take control or to make any real difference in his life. The individual in this mental state then strives for security rather than opportunity, and often feels like a victim of circumstances over which he has no control.

The only real limitation on what you can achieve is the level of intensity of your desire. If you really want something desperately enough, there are almost no limits on what you can achieve. And the more you learn about any subject, the greater will be your desire to accomplish something in that area. As your knowledge grows, you become more confident in taking the necessary steps to make your goals a reality. As you upsurge your levels of desire and knowledge, you decrease the self-limiting effects of fear and ignorance, and their companions, learned helplessness and the comfort zone. With desire and knowledge, you eventually substitute fear and ignorance with courage and confidence. The more you learn about anything that is important to you, the more courage you will have to attempt to achieve it, and the more confident you will be that you can eventually succeed.

We are living in a delightful world today, probably the best period in all of human history. You are encircled by more opportunities and possibilities to achieve your dreams than have ever existed before. There are no limits to what you can accomplish except for the limits that you put on yourself with your own thinking. The feeling of learned helplessness and the lure of the comfort zone are the two major mental obstacles to changing your thinking, dreaming big dreams, and setting big goals for yourself. The way to overcome fear and ignorance is with desire and knowledge. The two qualities that flow out of intense desire and increased knowledge are the courage and the confidence you need to do whatever is necessary to achieve anything you really want. Translate your dreams into concrete realities by turning them into goals. You decide exactly what you want, write it down, set a deadline, and determine the efforts you are going to have to make to achieve it. Make written plans of action to achieve your goal and then do something every day to move toward it. Resolve in advance that you will never, ever give up.

Forget the past, we all have had our fair share of disappointments in life, but don't live in the past, it has gone. So right now, resolve to be a new you, an individual who is determined to succeed and live life on your terms. Make this day a new beginning of a new adventure of greatness. It's time to get on your grind by focusing your mind on success. It is the mind that holds the majority of people back from going after what they truly want. The mind is what paralyzes people from taking action. Once you break down those mental barriers that have imprisoned you, you will live life differently, your perspective, your actions, your goals, your plans, your limits, and your fears will disappear. Success is not a sprint, it a marathon. Don't be a coward and remain confined to an average life. Fortunately, getting to the top is easier than you think. The great majority of people seldom think about personal excellence. And if the thought crosses their minds, they quickly dismiss it and go back to average performance. Most of the people around you are content to do their jobs, for better or for worse, and then go out with their friends, or go home and watch television. However, when you begin to make those extra efforts that enable you to excel, you will find that, like a runner going into a sprint, you soon move ahead of the pack of the average performers.

You can be a leader of your life and live life how you want to live it, on your terms. Successful people are in control of their lives. They possess the willpower, self-discipline and emotional intelligence to design a life they are proud of and it's because they take the time to learn how their mind operates and how best to use it to their advantage. Never do or refrain from doing something because you are concerned about what people might think about you. The fact is that nobody is even thinking about you at all so let go the past.

Wow! Its amazing coming this far. You are finally coming to the end of this book and I encourage you to not just finish hard, but also pick a life lesson from this book that will enable you to make a difference in life.

CHAPTER TWENTY-FOUR

MAKE THE VOW TO DO IT!

Looking back, makes you smart. Looking forward, makes you mature. Looking down, makes you wise. Looking Up, makes you strong. When everything seems to be going against you, remember that the airplane takes off against the wind, not with it ....

What value do you place on yourself? Have you ever taken an inventory or have you just said, "Well, I know I could do it if I would? I believe I can drive better than that person who is driving now." Or, "I believe I could create a machine." Or, "I could be this or I could be that." When are you going to be what you could be? Honestly, are you worth anything in your own estimation? Have you set a price on yourself? Have you set a price on your own ability, on your own time? What is your word worth to yourself? That is why I say make the vow now! A preacher once said, *"It is not where you are that matters but what have been deposited in you by your creator."*

When others count you out, count yourself in. What you do for yourself counts far more than all that others have done or can do for you. Let me tell you something important here. Two resources that you can never renew in life are time and your youth. Time and tide, they say wait for no one. The tickling of time never stops. It is always moving from morning to evening. As we grow time ensures that we move on. This reminded me of an audio recording that trended on the social media about a FIFA official who was banned for life from participating in any activity related to football. He said, *"as a leader if you don't move on, you will be moved away."* That is why if you have anything in mind to do in life you've got to do it now. It is never too late to succeed in life as long as time and opportunity are available.

The fact that running ahead mean you are *die until the rotten.* This is one of the football clubs others are of you doesn't late. *Never say bones are* the motto of popular local in Ghana.

> *"Some people want it to happen, some wish it would happen, others make it happen"*
> **Michael Jordan**

What they mean is that until the game is over never accept defeat. Time and opportunity are always available for you. Why not get hold of them now and bring out something worthwhile from them? You cannot predict tomorrow's events so never say I will do it tomorrow. I also remembered vividly what the wisest king who ever lived on earth said in Ecclesiastic 12:1 *"Remember your Creator in the days of your youth, before the days of trouble come and the years approach when you will say, "I find no pleasure in them."* Only those who dare to enter the unknown can know what is hidden there so arise and enter now.

Once you outgrow your youth no other period of youth would be credited to you. That is why you can't afford to mess up with your youthful age. Don't live your youth ages like how others are living. Everyone of us has his or her own path of life. Make good use of your youth now! Be conscious of every time you spent on any activity. If you are a student, be very meticulous of the amount of time you spent on your academic. As a business person or entrepreneur, be mindful of the time you waste on irrelevant things. I am very much aware that the youth of our time are more concerned about their social engagement. But let me be quick to add that don't let your social activities steal much of your academic and business life. We should **NOT** be a generation that is ready to defend the little they have; we are a generation whose eyes are fixed on the bigger picture.

Hear me, there is absolutely nothing you can do again on your own once you outgrow your youth. Your thinking patterns are very sharp in your youth but very low when you cross to old age. That is why I am repeating this to you my boss that think and act immediately in this stage of your youth. As you read through this line of words re-examine your thought processes and rise up to the top. I didn't come to look down on you. I came to whet your appetite to utilize your youthful exuberance. As youth you are free to choose your actions but you are not free to choose the consequences thereof. You are accountable to any action you undertake in life. Whether it is good or bad you will live to reap the result of that action. If you choose to stay at home doing nothing when your colleagues are busily working and making a living out of it then you will continually remain in your poverty.

Poverty will always knock at your door. In fact, poverty will totally be your best friend. That is why am saying make the vow now! Tell yourself enough of the sleeping! Enough of the complaining! The more you complain in life the more confused you will be in life. Enough of the blaming game! Open your creative mouth now and speak out what you want to become in the next day, week, month, and year. I want to hear you say it now. Say it my boss! Good! Now commit yourself to that vow and see what that outcome will be like. You can make it in life my boss. Let no one deceive you that there is no hope for you. That will be one of the greatest deceits the world will record. You can become that lawyer, doctor, nurse, teacher, professor, lecturer, that you dream of becoming in life. I see you rising up like an eagle in your education, in your career, and in your profession, in your business. Let the hard past of yours drive and push you to the top. I know your past is nothing to write home about, but believe you me its rather and energizing power meant to catapult you to the apex. The top where only brilliant and zealous people like you can reach. Set your mark; your standard; high. Then go up there. Allow no day to go by in which you have not improved yourself. You are too huge to depart from this earth without a memory in the sands of time.

Take an inventory again and again and see what you possess; see whether that possession is more valuable today than it was a year ago. Find where your ability lies. Then put all of your best into that ability and make that ability come across and put you over. Remember that what you have hungered and yearned to do; you have the ability to do; if you will. Come on don't think of the bottom. You don't belong to the bottom. You belong to the top. There is more space for you at the top than at the bottom. Soaring higher as an eagle is a natural phenomenon in your blue-print. Use it! You will pay nothing for using your mind but you become a debtor for not using it. Bellies of creation burn with hunger and hope of better days dwindle when you fail to amount to something in this life.

Refuse to be an average person. Have you ever asked yourself why lecturers and teachers like to obtain a normal curve when assessing the performance of their students? Let me tell you the reason. You see the normal curve assume that majority of the students stay in the middle of the curve while only few people stay at the two extreme ends. Those in the middle are said to have performed averagely while those in the extreme left and right are said to have performed poorly and excellently respectively. In this case, the teacher or lecturer now tend to praise those who performed excellently and then encourage those who performed poorly to do better. Have you realized from this case that the teacher or lecturer now pay no attention to the average students? Yes! When you choose to be an average person in life nobody will pay attention to you. My boss! I challenge you to push harder to become an excellent person in life.

The world is eagerly waiting for your manifestation. Make the vow now to rise up to the top. Speak to your inner man that you are meant for the top and not the bottom. Tell yourself you are the head and not the tail. It will be a serious disaster to allow your poor background to override your powerful life dreams. Within you lies the potential of the future president, minister, business gurus, cousellors, and many other professions you can think of. Never quit before the battle commence. Life is just a mocker. It frightens those who don't know their destination. So, keep fighting for what you believe. Keep going even if no one believe in you. Dare to utilize your heavenly endowered gifts before they expire. Say NO to everything that belittles your dream and entice your ego to complacency.

What is life about? You are standing on the threshold. Before you lie the untried paths. What are you going to do? Have you chosen your work, your vocation, your place in life, or are you drifting, hoping that something will turn up? It will, but the thing that turns up will be of no value to you unless you are ready to take it as it comes. Don't float. Dead fish float. Make up your mind that you will put your dreams into blue prints, and then, with that blue print in hand, you will build your mansion. Find your place, but be sure that you do thorough preparatory work. Put real hard work into the days of preparation. Don't just get by. Don't be satisfied with anything but one hundred plus. Fight for it. Work for it. Enjoy it. Make it a game to win.

Be a success in youth and you will be a success in middle life. You will be crowned in old age. Make yourself a wanted person. Be so valuable that if you had to move, men and women would weep because of your departure. If you plan to be a minister, be God's best. If you go into business, be the best in your community. If you plan to be a lawyer or a physician, put a trained, cultured personality into it. Whatever you do, plan to build your house on top of the hill. Harness that lazy mind and make it work. That mind can make a place for you. Let me say again to you, Go under your own steam. Prepare yourself, and doors will open to you everywhere.

Procrastination is not only the thief of time; it is the thief of life. To outperform your competition, both inside and outside your organization, you must develop the habit of moving *quickly* when something needs to be done. You must develop a reputation for speed and dependability. Study after study shows that those individuals with the best reputations for speed and dependability are the most valued in any organization. They are very quickly promoted onto the fast track in their careers. The wonderful advantage of developing the habit of moving fast is that the faster you move, the *better* you get. This is because the faster you move, the more experience you get. The faster you move, the more you learn and the more competent you become. The faster you move, the more energy and enthusiasm you have. People who move fast as a way of life soon develop a totally different temperament and personality than people who move slowly or who take a casual attitude toward their work.

Most people choose not to be rich. For majority of the population, being rich is too much of a hassle. So, they invent sayings that go: "I'm not interested in money." "I will never be rich." "I don't have to worry". "I'm still young." "When I make some money, then I will think about my future." "My husband/wife handles the finances." The problem with those statements is that they rob the person who chooses to think such thoughts of two things: One is time, which is your most precious asset. The second is learning. Having no money should not be an excuse to not learn. But that is a choice we all make daily: the choice of what we do with our time, our money, and what we put in our heads. That is the power of choice. All of us have choice. I just choose to read and write, and I make that choice every day.

Your most valuable asset is your time. It is also your scarcest resource. You have a limited amount of time, and once it is gone, it is gone forever. Time is essential to accomplishment. Time is perishable. You cannot get more of it, no matter what you do. It can be said that the quality of your life is determined by the way you spend this precious resource. Results and rewards, however you define them for yourself, are everything. Your ability to achieve the health, happiness, and prosperity you desire is the measure of your effectiveness as a human being. Your job is to use your minutes and hours more effectively to assure that you are achieving the greatest quantity and quality of the things you want in exchange for the time you invest.

You cannot save time. You can only spend it effectively. Every part of your life today shows the results of how you have spent your time in the past. If you want to have a different future, you have to spend your time differently in the present. You have to change your thinking about yourself and how you use your time to get the things you want in life. Time, in a way, is like *money*. It can be either spent or invested. If you spend time or money, it is gone forever. You can never get it back. But if you invest your time or money wisely, you will get a greater return in the future. Personal strategic planning and thinking give you the tools to ensure that you achieve the highest return on time invested. Put in another way, it enables you to get the highest "return on life."

Everything you do that necessitates your time represents a choice. The choice is to use your time wisely or not. However. you choose, the time will be gone forever. If you spend your time on one activity, you will no longer have that same quantity of time available to spend or invest in another activity. Your choices about how you use your time largely determine the quality of your life, both today and in the future. You must be extremely jealous of your time. You must be adamant about not spending your time on activities of low value.

You must downsize, outsource, and remove all activities that no longer represent the highest and best use of your time if you want to get the highest return on energy in your life and career as well as make a great difference in life. Zero-based thinking will help you to make better choices. It is a key thinking tool that can change your life.

THE END.

APPRECIATION

I want to specially congratulate you for taking your time to read this novel. Indeed, it wasn't an easy journey but you proved beyond all reasonable doubt that you are ready to make a difference and become successful in life.

I hope you really enjoyed yourself. If you do then let others hear about it by recommending this book to them.

Other services rendered by the author include:

1. **Inspirational talk**

2. **Presentations on:**
   ✓ Leadership
   ✓ Self-development
   ✓ Setting life goals
   ✓ Making a difference
   ✓ Becoming successful
   ✓ Harnessing the mind into wealth

   Target groups
   ✓ Schools
   ✓ Churches
   ✓ Organizations
   ✓ Individuals

Mobile No: **0248759578**
Email: **domaleyvincent7@gmail.com**

Arise and Make a Difference; the Drive Behind Success